AF301880

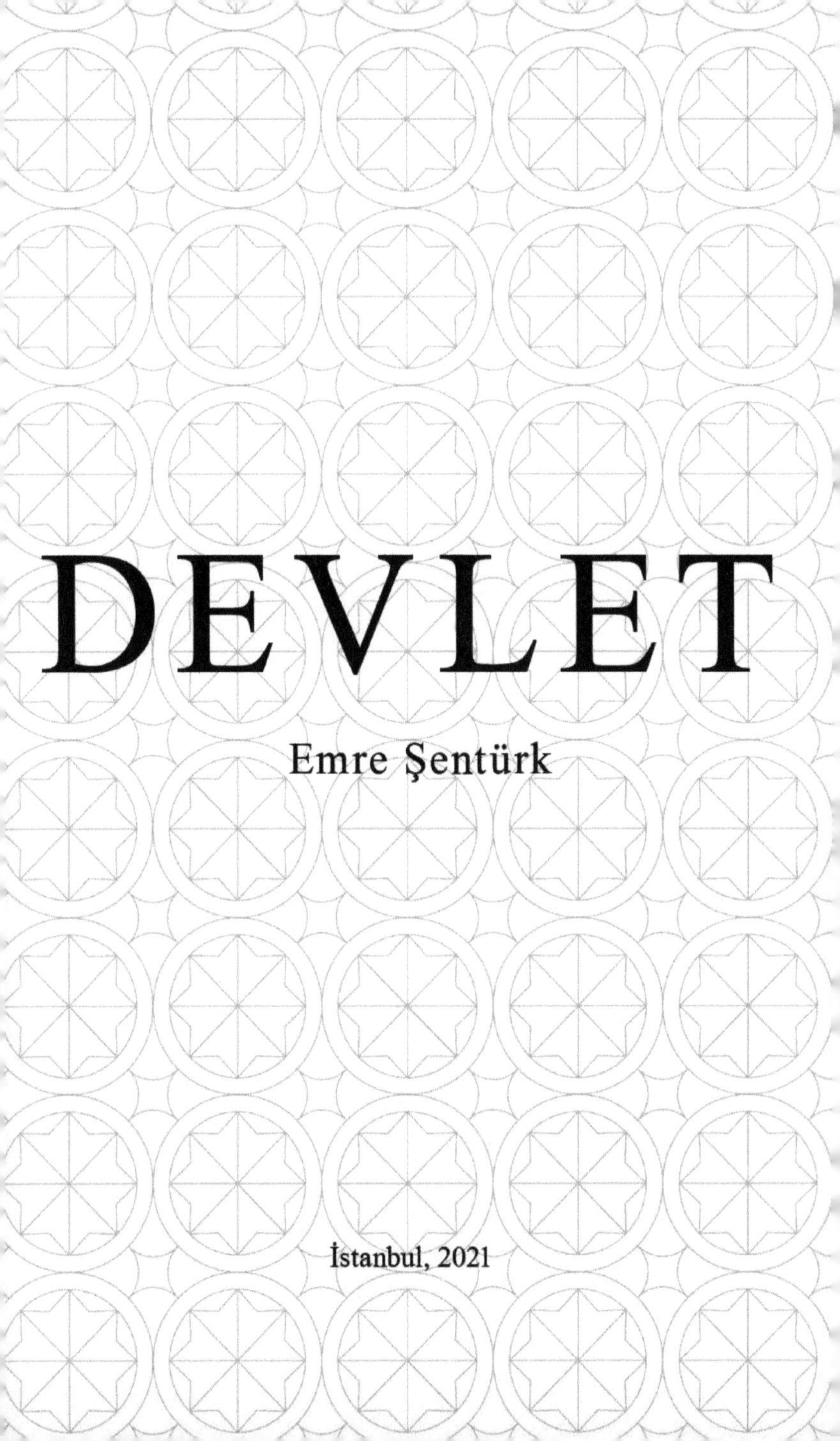

DEVLET

Emre Şentürk

İstanbul, 2021

Table of Contents

Prologue

Mankind's most important questions centre around the organisation of our lives within societies. Although countless scholars, philosophers and politicians have invested vast amounts of energy and time in making sense of the way of our societal organisation, we seem to have made very little progress in relation to the century-old efforts that we have put into advancing as a species. Of course, there are underlying agendas and interests – among many other factors – that hinder effective and efficient progress. Moreover, it might well be a misconception on my part to think that we have the necessary knowledge to transform our societies in a way that is aligned with the purpose of life. However, I defend that our societies function far below their true potential – not because we do not want to, but because the structures simply guide us into this inefficiency. The main problem is that we are unaware of what we are doing on this planet and why we do it. At the very best, our current goals are limited in their usefulness and reaching those goals will lead us to a dead end if we continue to move in the direction of said goals. This holds true for our personal lives, the societies we live in and the politics that guides our societies.

I believe that the philosophical background of much of the work produced until today is insufficient to understand a state's purpose and hence, its role. It is needless to say that all philosophical assumptions limit the production of intellectual work; even having no assumptions is a limiting attitude in its own way. We can compare this to a journey to an unfamiliar place. Having a map is useful to reach the destination, but the map would be useless if it depicts a different country. However, not having a map does not increase our chances of reaching the destination, either. To get where we want to be, we must first be sure that we have the right tools to get there. But before that, it is necessary to identify our destination. Politics should be functioning in the same way. There should be clarity about the purpose of our existence and then what is needed to get there. Politics is the institutional vehicle that helps us fulfil this purpose by means of organising societal conduct.

This might be easy in theory, but in terms of practicability, there are significant obstacles grounded in the complexity of our societies as well as in the misconception of what political systems should do for them. In this work, I propose a new state theory which reaches beyond the limitations of our current political understanding. The theory is named 'Devletism', originating from the Turkish word for *state*. I define it as:

> *A form of societal organisation that aims for joint and continuous progression through the advancement of genuine knowledge.*

Beginning with the philosophical underpinnings of this new school of state theory, I aim to rectify our understanding of a political system's purpose that naturally stems from our purpose as individual human beings.

During the process of writing this treatise, some of the people I have talked to have described the ideas in this work as a utopia. I would not go that far. In essence, this work proposes just a minor readjustment of focus. While I reject previous philosophical assumptions about our individual purpose in life – and with them the perception of the purpose of political systems – I would not have been able to develop the devletist idea without the works of past great minds. The devletist idea is, hence, just a logical continuation of past achievements, which are limited in providing future guidance from this point onwards due to the different societal circumstances of our time. A time might come when Devletism also becomes insufficient to provide guidance to individuals, societies and states. However, it can serve as an important building block for the workings of future scholars, politicians, philosophers and any other person who aims to improve our existence on this planet and maybe even on other planets. The purpose of this work is to establish a state philosophy capable of elevating our societies to a higher standard of living and, most importantly, increasing the quality of life without, paradoxically, these material goals constituting the ends of policy actions. This will be picked up later in greater detail.

On a more personal note, I would like to thank all the valuable people in my life for the opportunity to learn from them. I would like to express my gratitude for all the support, discussions and motivation I received from those who believed in me and the value of my work. Moreover, I would also like to express my deepest love and admiration to all political scientists who continuously add to the advancement of our beautiful field of science. And to the great political minds and hands of the past, who have shaped what we call history.

Chapter I

Philosophical Foundations

A thought is like a plant. Just like a plant needs soil and water to exist, a thought needs a philosophical foundation and constant contact with the world to grow. If it happens that this thought can be entertained throughout a variety of different settings in our reality, it strengthens its right to exist. The more a thought can survive tests against real world scenarios, the more authoritative the core premises of this thought. This also means that the soil from which this thought arises, the philosophical foundation, must be an equally sustainable system. Similarly, when a thought or belief system (philosophical foundation) successfully tests against different settings in the real world constantly, it can be thought to encompass great portions of what we call the truth. Now, the truth is a particularly difficult concept and, as such, subject to much debate. Some claim that the truth is not absolute but relative or subjective. Viewing the truth as something flexible or subjective is a philosophical foundation in itself. Thoughts that are born out of this view are likely to produce meaningful results only in the light of this view that the truth is subjective. It makes it difficult to compare this ontology to other philosophical foundations with different ontological assumptions. Nonetheless, there needs to be a discussion on the nature of the truth. Here, it is defended that there is an objective truth. This view is not new.[1] However, many argue that this objective truth cannot be perceived in its natural form since people view the world in different ways. Although the latter is undeniably true, it does not conflict with the notion that there is an objective truth. We could, for example, say that the fact that people view the world differently is an integral part of the true reality. Or we could argue that the different perspectives arise from a lacking awareness of the concept of objective truth. Both ideas are compatible with the assumption that there is a universal objective truth. Such a truth is not affected by the different beliefs people hold on what is true or not, while the objective truth could be one that has a place for those different beliefs on the truth.

On the other hand, arguing that there is no such objective truth but only many different true individual realities creates a direct conflict between the two ontological views as it does not allow both to coexist. This is because the relative approach treats each subjectively constructed reality as a fully independent entity in its own right, ascribing a validity to each and every perceived reality that needs to be accepted. On this ground, adopting the idea that there is an objective truth would infringe the validity of

---

[1] First structured thoughts about the nature of truth can be traced back to Socrates. In Plato's *Republic,* in the dialogue between Thrasymachus and Socrates, it becomes clear that he refers to only one truth, even on a normative topic like justice.

the subjective truths. Another shortcoming of this thinking is an implicit dependency on the truth. What happens to this subjective truth without human beings? It is hard to argue that truth as a concept ceases to be without the existence of humans or other consciously reflecting organisms. It follows that humans can hold different views on the world but cannot claim that those views and beliefs are true if they are not representative of the objective truth. This finding mainly illustrates the existence of the concepts of "right" and "wrong", which has significant implications for the judiciary of the devletist state.

Again, the absolute approach, too, allows those differently perceived realities to exist. They are situated hierarchically under the overarching umbrella of the universal truth. Such an approach does not conflict with the notion that there are different perceptions of the world; there can be a multitude of different perceived realities without changing the properties of the objective truth. It also does not reduce the validity of subjective perceptions but subordinates them to the objective truth. Hence, this encompassing view that there is, indeed, an objective truth is more powerful than the opposing ontological assumption of the subjective truth.

Next, some could argue that even if there is such an objective truth, it would not be possible for us to fully reveal it. However, we as human beings can technically perceive and even understand this objective truth, so I claim. Our species might not be able to do so today, but in countless millennia in the future. This does not make current human efforts to advance obsolete since these are necessary steps to moving closer to understanding the objective truth. I go even further by saying that we ought to understand this objective truth. Reaching this understanding of the objective truth of the universe is the sole purpose of every organism's existence. We shall shortly see why.

In search for the answer to the question as to why this is the ultimate purpose of our, and every other species', existence, we can use hypothetical thought experiments to single out this question's answer from a wide array of philosophical views on this question.[2] We could imagine that there is only one human being left on this planet. Said human knows she is the only human and there will not be another human being while she exists. What would be a meaningful driving factor of her behaviour? Next to sustaining her life by searching for water and food, her lonely existence must also consist of activities that require her to use the extended consciousness that humans possess – in comparison towards plants and animals, which they do not have yet. Without social contacts, the factors of love and friendship are useless in providing answers to what would influence her behaviour. The

---

[2] This method is a more suitable approach to questions of this complexity. Though thought experiments seldom provide a fully sufficient answer, they can direct the cognitive efforts towards the potential answer, as it was the case with *Schrödinger's Cat.*

only exception might be seeking closeness to animals and spending time with them, but communication and sharing of experiences would be limited and, thus, not fulfilling. Seeking enjoyment in visiting beautiful places or engaging in thrilling activities are equally weak explanations of what would drive behaviour here because these activities will, at some point, lose their positive effect on the psyche of our last human being. For one, they will become repetitive and purposeless, but there is also nobody to share those experiences with. The only activity that can be continuously exercised without seizing to be interesting is to gain knowledge and, hence, move closer to an understanding of the objective truth. With or without other humans, the essence of knowledge production remains the same. It does not gain more importance within a society than it does without one. The accumulation of knowledge is independent and inexhaustible because knowledge itself exists independently. No organism is bound to another organism to explore the truth. Having support from others can surely add to the efficiency of the process, but it does not constitute a necessity. Therefore, knowledge is unconditionally independent. If we assume that there is, indeed, a purpose for our existence, then it must be something that exists independently and is not tied to the condition that there are other organisms that would make the existence of other purposes, such as love and friendship, possible. Every human action, except for one, depends on the existence of, or interaction with, other human beings. Either we need them to engage in the action in the first place, or they are necessary for the action to become meaningful. The only action that does not require such a constellation is knowledge production. Since knowledge production is the only human action that exists independently, it must be the sole purpose of our existence.

In the context of politics, we can think about similar scenarios. Every political system, to my knowledge, was either concerned with gaining more power – diplomatically, economically or militarily, or all three of them – or with increasing the material comfort of its society. In the case of power, let us think about a nation that was able to conquer the entire world. What would happen next? Surely, the goal then would be to maintain this status quo, but even when this situation can be maintained for centuries, a question as to what the driving factor of all subsequent acts would be would arise. Well, we could say that the ruler of the political system would then try to conquer other planets and galaxies and let us suppose that she was able to do so, too. What would happen next? What would be a meaningful motivation for her behaviour? There is nothing meaningful we could think of because the actions, until this point, were aimed at reaching this situation. But no agenda guides behaviour beyond that. It follows that power considerations are exhaustible and, therefore, cannot serve as a basis for understanding the purpose of states.

The same logic can be applied when considering the aspect of wealth. Let us imagine that the entire world has reached such a level of material comfort that every person lives in excessive luxury and has no material concerns. How would our behaviour change? What would drive subsequent behaviour in such an environment? Here again, reaching such a goal would lead the political system to a dead end because there is nothing more to achieve since everyone is already living in ultimate luxury. In both examples, reaching their goals would end their existence because they can, in theory, be reached. This is not the case with knowledge, which makes pursuing knowledge significantly more superior to pursuing power or wealth and comfort. A political system concerned with reaching a better understanding of the universe will never run into a dead end because there will always be questions that reach beyond the acquired pool of knowledge without becoming less relevant than the answers to the previous questions. Even what is believed to be known will often turn out to be untrue and require re-evaluation. It follows that the purpose of our existence must be centred around the search and development of knowledge and not around increasing power or wealth and comfort.

Why is this important? Let us return to our plant and its soil and water. This work establishes a new state theory – this is the thought and metaphorically the plant. To understand the nature of this thought, we need to see under which conditions it came into existence. The philosophical foundation in which this state theory is grounded is what was described above: the objective truth and our purpose of existence tied to it. The purpose of every organism's existence is to work towards the understanding of the objective truth. Because this is the main assumption of why we exist, it is only natural that the proposed state system must be designed to realise this purpose of existence effectively and efficiently.[3] Compared to previous assumptions that state purpose is built around increasing wealth and power, this view provides a meaningful normative framework for statecraft.

And what about the water? Just like a plant needs to be constantly fed with water, a thought needs to be fed with different situations from our reality. The analogy is a little bit off – I admit – since a plant consumes water to grow, but a thought is tested against different situations to prove that it can survive. Throughout this work, there will be arguments put forward, claiming that devletist systems can survive these situations and provide a better ground for our species to fulfil the purpose of our existence.

Now that the main guiding thought is clearly defined, the question, naturally, arises as to how we as a species can work towards this understanding of the objective truth. The answer to

---

[3] It can, and also should, be followed that the design of all political systems, past or present, reflect the underlying assumptions by their founders and supporters about our purpose of existence.

that is that we can achieve this through *genuine knowledge production.* Genuine knowledge production is not as straightforward as it might sound at first. Surely, scientific advances, which are probably among the first things that come to our minds, are part of it, but they are neither the sole nor the main factor that this concept is built on. Here, we need to understand other assumptions in the first place.

Every human has a special trait that lies at the deepest point of a person's subconscious. Some might call it talent, purpose, gift or destiny. But they all describe roughly the same thing. This special trait develops in the very early stages of our biological existence and arguably even before that.[4] What is important is that every person needs to find this very point in her subconscious, become familiar with it and internalise an awareness of it. It is a recurring theme throughout philosophy as great thinkers pointed out that one must, before anything else, know herself.[5] Some followed that this is the key to success, while others linked it to love or other emotions and goals. Within

---

[4] Within the *nature-nurture-debate*, which the question about the special trait needs to be located in, I tend to side with the emergenic view.

[5] Not only is this a recurring theme in Western philosophy ("Know thyself" being inscribed at the Temple of Delphi, according to the writer Pausanias, 10.24.1. Over the centuries, it was picked up in the teachings of Plato, René Descartes or Thomas Hobbes) but also in Islamic and East-Asian teachings. Islamic teachings of this notion have been influenced by Ibn Arabi and Jalal al-Din Muhammad Rumi who tied the idea of self-knowledge to the religion of Islam. In the Chinese history, Lao Tzu also treats self-knowledge as an essential attribute of wisdom (Tao Te Ching, ch. 33).

the framework of the philosophy of this work, this special trait needs to be found because it enables one to work in this field with a significant unquantifiable advantage. For example, we can think about a doctor who simply has "a hand" for her profession, while others study this craft for decades and cannot match the level of knowledge and understanding that the talented doctor has. The reason is that the doctor has lived through a genuine and honest development process and happened to find this special trait at the deepest point of her character. By finding and developing this trait, one engages in genuine knowledge production as one works on fulfilling her purpose of existence. As mentioned earlier, this is not solely confined to the sciences but to virtually any area of our lives. Whether it is sports, music, art, literature or a certain craft, every person has this special trait, which can come in any form. Once found and developed, the outcome of the work will always be positive, though the path towards the outcome may be demanding. This is the point where genuine knowledge production happens. And where it happens, our species moves one step closer to understanding the objective truth that guides our universe because people with unquantifiable advantages seek to improve the state of art within their field. Society advances.

This is the thought system from which Devletism arose and in which devletist state systems will be embedded in. It follows that devletist systems need to be designed in ways that enable its people to discover themselves and also provide them with the opportunity to translate their potential into outcomes. The reason why devletist systems aim to do this is because there is the underlying premise that our species must move closer to the full understanding of the objective truth. By providing an environment that removes as many barriers as possible to finding and utilising every person's special trait, everyone can add to societal progress in the most effective and efficient way, which is then accelerated through an accumulative effect at the societal level. Today, politics is unaware of this objective truth and, hence, cannot effectively work towards understanding it. How can you move towards something if its existence is unknown to you?[6]

Contemporary systems are based on approaches that lean heavily on power aspirations, personal and collective material desires and short-term thinking. Devletism challenges this order by designing politics in a way that makes whole societies work efficiently on societal progress by enabling personal development in the first place. Devletism's biggest challenges are managing individual and aggregate level development, international influences and decadent societal tendencies. Many

---

[6] It does not categorically exclude societal or personal advancement in which the society or person is unfamiliar with the devletist teachings. However, consciousness about these concepts or closely related notions significantly adds to the effectiveness of progress.

of the specific material structures of the political system, which will be described throughout the rest of this work, will inevitably collapse at a certain point in time as we progress as a species. Voting procedures, governance structures and institutions will lose relevance in a couple of centuries – as they should. These kinds of policy structures are useful to elevate societies from their current status quo to the next stage of development but are not meant to stay in place forever. However, the philosophical underpinnings should withstand time because the purpose of existence, which was described before, is a constant. So, it is necessary to understand that the workable measures in this work are tailored to this day and age. But once these structures start to hamper societal progression, the necessary changes must be implemented, again, based on the assumption that our species must collectively move towards a better understanding of the objective truth. The longer this philosophical assumption can survive societal and political change, the more authoritative it is going to become. Hopefully, the assumption that our existence is centred around understanding the functioning of our universe is going to survive many centuries and will guide our species through changes and hardships, while the ways in which we aim to achieve this will adapt to become more effective and efficient.

Chapter II

The Purpose of States

The study of the state is one of the oldest sciences. Many philosophers, politicians and scientists tried to make sense of how we, as a species, organise ourselves in large groups. While we are capable of producing a common sense of identity around specific sets of values, symbols, myths and languages, we are comparatively unable to sustainably agree on how to organise societies. One structural finding that has withstood time are the teachings of Aristotle, who found a useful categorisation of forms of political rule. He said that a state can be ruled by one person, a group of few people or by the whole society, which is under the jurisdiction of the state. These are the only three ways societies can be governed.

It needs to be said that there is no inherent difference in quality between them.[7] Rather than the form of political rule, the guiding premises of political behaviour are key. There are a few guiding themes that scholars have built their state theories on. One prominent theme is the theme of survival. Some scholars argue that our need to survive is the most fundamental instinct and,

---

[7] Aristotle´s distinction between "right" and "perverted" forms of the three types of government are not considered here. I only refer to the technical categorisation regarding the quantity of rulers. It surely is right to assume that the misuse of power will in any case alter the character of the political system.

hence, the strongest factor that motivates our behaviour. While the former is definitely true, the latter is not. Surely, our survival instinct is our most fundamental instinct, and it is every state's responsibility to secure its citizens', as well as its own, survival – otherwise, any other purposes cannot be fulfilled. However, it is not the most crucial factor that guides our behaviour, and it surely is not the sole purpose of our existence. Scholars who base their political teachings on the argument that the states' behaviour is solely motivated by survival considerations claim that states aim to increase their power towards other states. This has the effect that it defers much less powerful states from becoming a threat to the own state's survival. Further, it increases the chances of withstanding aggressions from more powerful states. It does not mean that these conflicts arise solely on a military basis, as we can think about power in economic and cultural terms, too.

Now, all these thoughts hold great portions of truth, but viewing politics in this way has a major shortcoming, as we have also seen in the previous chapter. It solely describes political processes and provides one understandable yet limited explanation of them. However, we cannot derive any added value from viewing politics this way. It is not even possible to reliably predict state behaviour on this basis. We can only use this approach in hindsight to say that, for instance, state A attacked, diplomatically isolated or sanctioned state B in order to improve its power position towards this actor or towards other actors. It helps us, to a limited extent, to understand what has happened, but little more than that. Considerations of survival are purely reactionary, as actions in the light of power considerations are dependent on other states' actions and inactions, while genuine knowledge production exists independently at any given moment. To understand a state's behaviour from the perspective of power, actions by at least one other state are necessary to be considered since power is measured against the power of others. And because this is the case, even positive developments do not stem from an intrinsic motivation to advance but from the perception that this development is needed to influence a power relationship. Thus, the concept of power does not provide a proactive agenda that would help us understand state behaviour and is even limiting our thinking by reducing state behaviour to a two-dimensional relational scope.

Another and equally common form of viewing the state, its purpose and approaching the study of state behaviour is the notion of peace and comfort. Rather than merely seeking to survive, a state should, proponents of this school say, provide its citizens with an environment of peace and prosperity.[8] This approach is normative. It requires a state to behave proactively

---

[8] Jean-Jacques Rousseau, in his work *The Social Contract,* states: "What is the purpose of any political association? The preservation and prosperity of its members".

and seek ways to make life more comfortable for its own citizens
– even if it is at the expense of other societies. Here, we have a
different philosophical approach to the question of our existence.
Usually, scholars of this school would assume that peace is an
end in itself and would often define it as the absence of war,
famine, poverty, crime and other disasters.[9] In their view, a
state's purpose is to achieve and sustain this situation. Therefore,
it is assumed that the state would behave in suitable ways to
achieve just that. If we hypothetically assume that this situation
is reached, then the question of what would happen next remains,
which we have also looked at earlier. In such a situation, there is
no meaningful driver of our behaviour. Also, we have always had
the resources and means to reach this level for the entire
population of the world but never reached this situation. But even
if, why would we go to work when we have perfect peace and
live in excessive comfort? Why would we engage in science?
There is no purpose in doing so. The answer, in that case, would
be self-fulfilment. But also, in the light of self-fulfilment, some
questions arise. Why would a scientist then continue within her
field and not pursue something else? Why would the artist
continue to do what she does and not do something else? The

---

[9] Many scholars emphasised the importance of normative constructs for peace,
such as justice. Due to potential definitional discrepancies with such scholars, I
avoided enlisting normative concepts, though I acknowledge that they play a role
in their understanding of peace. Undeniably though, they all view the condition
of peace as an essential goal for society, regardless of how one would define it.

answer is that people's behaviour is guided by their special trait. Accordingly, the purpose of our existence, once again, must be the genuine production of knowledge grounded in the existence of our special trait, our struggle to find it and ultimately, our desire to produce outcomes in this field. This can happen infinitely without losing its core characteristic and requiring a context.

From this, it follows that a state's purpose is to provide an environment for the effective and efficient production of genuine knowledge. Surely, survival, power, peace and prosperity are all important aspects that influence states' behaviour to some degree, and they surely have some explanatory capacity, but they are all not the true purposes of states. These are all by-products of a state that mainly focuses on providing an environment for the effective and efficient production of genuine knowledge. By not focusing on these lower tiers of factors, they become routine tasks for the state and enable it to advance more quickly. Think about a musician who tries to become famous: her success will always lag behind a musician who is exclusively concerned with perfecting her craft. Of course, without survival, there would be no genuine knowledge production, and without peace and comfort, there would be great barriers to the effective and efficient development of the nation. However, looking beyond those aspects of statecraft, they will naturally be part of the state.

This is the main difference between the devletist school of thought and other schools treating the state. Rather than standing in conflict with those concepts, Devletism leaves room for them and encompasses them, while they, in turn, fail to encompass Devletism. Again, a hierarchy between the existing schools and devletist thoughts is visible, as they put exhaustible considerations above the inexhaustible goal of the devletist school. This makes Devletism a superior school when we reflect on the tests of philosophical foundations. It answers the question of what a state's purpose is, while the other schools cannot.

Viewing the state in such a light has important implications for the design of the state, its institutions, its behaviour and the way it manages societal conduct. Contemporary democratic systems are based on the premise that a state ought to provide safety, prosperity and comfort to its citizens. What looks like a convenient agenda at first leads to serious problems in reality. Decadency is the result of societal life becoming more centred around economic conduct. Life is degraded to a continuous consumption cycle because this is the main ingredient of our understanding of comfort. The mode of knowledge production faces a grave goal displacement under such conditions as scientific progress is driven by economic instead of intrinsic concerns. It does not mean that Devletism despises wealth and prosperity. In fact, devletist systems have the potential to achieve sustainable prosperity at unprecedented heights. Through the production of genuine knowledge, the quality of production and innovation increases, while economic conduct becomes more efficient. In a devletist system, products, for example, would need to be produced in a way that makes them last a very long time because it is produced to fulfil a purpose. The longer it can fulfil this purpose under the toughest conditions, the closer it reflects the state of art in producing this good. This means that only high-quality materials can be used, and the replacement rate of products decreases. Moreover, it means that waste and other harmful by-products and inefficiencies are reduced. The products in circulation become extremely high quality, increasing the standard of living for everyone. Later, the economy in devletist systems will be analysed in further detail.

Again, what differentiates Devletism from the other schools of political thought, is that it believes that neither survival nor peace or material wealth provides the proper basis for state behaviour. A state needs to achieve genuine knowledge production. In order to do that, it needs to survive, and peace is the condition under which the mode of production can happen, while wealth is a facilitating factor. However, these aspects are in no way ends in themselves but rather means to achieve higher collective societal goals.

Chapter III

About the Centrality of Culture

Before embarking on the endeavour to explore the specifics of the devletist state. It is necessary to define the following key terms: *culture, society, nation, state* and *government.* These are the recurrent concepts that will be used throughout this work. Hence, avoiding confusion of those concepts in the attempt to fully grasp the devletist thought is all the more important. The concepts are heavily interrelated and even interdependent, except for the concept of culture, as this is the building block for all the following concepts. It follows that this is the central term that requires special attention.

Culture is a term that describes a set of social interactions within an ethnic group. But to better understand the term, it is necessary to explore how cultures come into existence. Let us envision an unpopulated territory. Every territory is unique and, therefore, has unique properties. For organisms to live there, they need to adapt to the specifics of the territory. This holds true for humans just as much as it holds true for plants and animals, which is the reason why we have different types of plants and animals spread across our planet but also different ethnicities among human beings. However, the influence of nature on us is not only confined to our phenotypical characteristics but also affects our minds. Phenotypical characteristics are much harder to influence than psychological characteristics, and if those phenotypical characteristics adapt to our environment, we can reasonably expect that our minds, too, adapt to the environment.[10] Mediated are those influences mainly through the instinctive mode of survival considerations, which force us to shape our behaviour in accordance with how the territory is structured.

The population of an island lives fundamentally differently than a group of people that lives in the mountains. Because the island population is likely to rely on fishing and potentially be exposed to higher temperatures, they will develop different innovations but also have a different cognitive connection to their surroundings. It influences the way they perceive the world and how their social interactions are structured. For example, the amount and composition of different nutritional resources affect the level of cooperation and sense of community. If there are abundant food sources, the population is less likely to cooperate and has a lower sense of belonging as the level of dependency within the members of the group is lower. However, if the mode of obtaining these resources is more difficult, more cooperation is necessary. In areas with less abundant food sources, the cooperation and sense of belonging is higher, but the level of

---

[10] Darwin, Charles. *On the Origin of Species by Means of Natural Selection, or Preservation of Favoured Races in the Struggle for Life*. London: John Murray, 1859.

hostility between different groups is higher, too, as they are more likely to see each other as threats to their own survival since they compete for the same scarce resources. These are only a few examples, and it is not the aim here to derive rules for the effects of the surroundings on societies. Such examples, however, are useful to illustrate the uniqueness of every territory and how its unique composition is also the reason for the uniqueness of cultures.

In any case, language is a central aspect of cultures. No matter how the influences translate into reality, they have the effect that ethnic groups develop a common language to manage social conduct through communication. While language is a socially constructed phenomenon, it is, first and foremost, the result of the aggregate influences of the geographical specifics of a certain territory. Also, spiritual views, customs and traditions are products of this environment. It is often difficult to single out which geographical factor led to what kind of behaviour and how that behaviour, in turn, led to the emergence of specific languages, traditions and mentalities. However, this is not relevant to understand culture as a term.[11] Culture is rather used to refer to a specific set of behaviour and language. With the

---

[11] How certain factors could probably lead to the emergence of different traits and characteristics is not important here insofar their specifics do not alter the use of the term culture within this work. Albeit such a discussion would be enriching in many other contexts.

specifics of a certain territory, a group is, therefore, not only phenotypically similar due to the same natural influences, but they are forced to display similar behavioural patterns in order to ensure their survival within that territory. While an ethnic group is merely a group that shares highly similar genetic properties, culture is the term that summarises the unique set of behavioural patterns of that group, but not the ethnic group itself.

Turning to the concept of society, it can be seen as a more developed stage of culture. Here, the similar cultures of smaller communities within an ethnic group are connected through a common sense of belonging. This sense of belonging requires awareness of the similarities between these communities. A society, therefore, is a term that provides more structure to the understanding of our conduct within an ethnic group. Returning to the example of the island population, we can reasonably assume that the whole population is ethnically highly similar, if not equal. Let us assume that there are different smaller communities spread across the island. Because they are subject to the same natural influences which requires them to alter their behaviour accordingly, they will develop similar patterns of behaviour, social interaction and communication – and even similar spiritual views. In short, they will be culturally highly homogeneous, even if they developed independently on that island. Now, we can describe the way they behave, talk and think with the term culture. However, only when all of the communities meet and start extending their intragroup conduct to the whole island population can we speak of a society here. It requires that the groups become aware of their similarities and produce a sense of belonging that fosters the strengthening of ties among the groups. Thus, society describes an ethnic population with a shared culture.

Culture and society are universal concepts. Every ethnic group has a culture, and many highly similar ethnic groups have developed into societies. Often, those groups are viewed as one ethnic group over time. Nevertheless, it does not follow that they will also become a nation. This is the third concept that we need to look at. A nation is the institutionalised and materially consolidated form of a society. This means that nations have distinct boundaries and retain sovereignty over that territory, with the society as its population.[12] In essence, the nation is an abstract construct because it is basically the intra-societal institutionalisation of the common identity through a process of material unity and distinction towards the rest of the world. Other than the concept of society, which is inherently inward-looking, the construct of the nation is outward-looking as it authoritatively claims exclusiveness of its designated territory. In the case of our island society, it would mean that the groups with the common

---

[12] These points lean on Article 1 of the Montevideo Convention on the Rights and Duties of States (1933).

culture – which already became a society through the common sense of belonging – decide they have exclusive authority over the island. For a nation to claim such a space on this planet, it naturally needs to be respected by other societies and nations since no territorial space can be exclusively claimed by two societies or nations simultaneously.

There can only be one nation within the boundaries of a certain territory, but there can be more than one society within a certain territory, even if it is designated as a nation of another society.[13] In political terms, we call this acceptance of a nation by the rest of the world *recognition*.[14] Societies do not need recognition because they are not materially consolidated. They do not have a legal persona. Nations, in turn, are legal persons due to their sovereignty claim. National anthems, flags, myths and a common history strengthen the intra-societal awareness of the nation as they are meaningful symbols of the abstract concept of the nation. They are born out of the cultural specifics and societal dynamics. These aspects constitute the material part of the societal identity, which then becomes the visible facet of the national identity. However, these do not suffice for the proper administration and functioning of the society as a nation.

---

[13] Many nations host a great number of different societies, though the nation stems from one society.

[14] This concept is neither clearly defined nor unanimously agreed on. Even less so is this concept coherently applied as recognition has a horizontal and a vertical dimension.

Institutions are the material components of the nation. They are necessary to administer the proper functioning of the different parts of societies. In devletist terms, they provide the mechanism for the nation to realise genuine knowledge production. The whole of the institutions and their interrelation is called the state. The state is subordinate to the idea of the nation that embodies the cultural specifics in the form of a consolidated identity and is recognised by the rest of the world. While the state needs to adhere to the principles of the nation, it also provides the necessary structure for the nation to uphold its territorial claim, societal functioning and protection of its population and it is the mediating factor that enables the recognition by the rest of the world. Just like the bones are subordinate to the will of the brain, they provide the necessary structure for the body to function.

Finally, let us turn to the government. It is located at the lowest end of the hierarchy of these concepts. It is subordinate to the culture, the society, the nation and the state. It is merely a cadre of people who work within the state institutions and is bound to act according to the interests and principles of the nation. They are replaceable servants of the nation. Albeit, their quality eventually determines the quality of societal advancement.

Chapter IV

About the Use of Devletism

A devletist state is a technocratic state. Regardless of whether the form is monarchic, aristocratic or democratic, the functioning of the state needs to be on a technical basis at all times. This implies that the structures outlined in this work are not meant to be viewed as the blueprint of the perfect state. Since we are subject to constant change, the systems we build to organise societal life need to change, too. We need to understand this to be able to view political systems properly and extract maximum value from statesmanship. Political systems must be approached without emotional attachment. Today, we tend to think that democracies, in their current form, constitute the pinnacle of political systems, but one day, they, too, will be antiquated. The state structures in this work are designed to find application in today's environment and aim to provide a systemic structure into which we can easily transform our current states. Furthermore, they also pave the way for more efficient system adaptations in the future. For example, the proposed state here is a democratic one, but it does not follow that devletist systems always need to be democratic.

The important thing to keep in mind is that it is neither the institutions nor the people that defines what a devletist system is or is not. It is rather the question about whether the system enables the society to advance through a process of genuine knowledge production effectively and efficiently, at all times. Based on our experience with us as a species and the political systems we have created and destroyed over time, this work addresses current structural weaknesses and poses an alternative governing structure which will help us achieve societal progress. Once in place, new problems will arise and pose challenges to the states' aim of genuine knowledge production, which Decletism should overcome with its effective core premises. First, it is important that the devletist idea becomes the normative standard in the discussion about a state's purpose. If we internalise that a state's purpose is to enable its society to pursue genuine knowledge production effectively and efficiently, then the way in which it happens is secondary. Accordingly, the core innovations, while being novel, are not the material structures laid out here but the assumptions that they are grounded in.

However, just as humans today are fighting over which way is the best to achieve a happier and more prosperous society, we will fight in the future about how to achieve a (or the best) societal environment for genuine knowledge production, while all the different camps within this discussion will claim that they have found the right way to achieve this. The philosophical foundation of Devletism, as we remember, is that there is one objective truth. This implies that there is an objective truth about the perfect condition for this mode of production under the specific situation that we are in now or in the future. The proposed state structures try to move as close as possible to this truth about what would be the best way in the contemporary situation to achieve effective and efficient knowledge production. Unfortunately, there is no way we can know beforehand how close this system would be to the ideal contemporary devletist political system. Once implemented, however, the devletist dynamics of the system will inherently push it to improve going forward. Furthermore, this reads as if all political systems are identical, which is certainly not reflective of the reality, as we should also see in detail later. In this work, contemporary democratic systems are broadly generalised, while the main state structure, which was used as a point of reference for the policy proposals, is the Republic of Türkiye. Nonetheless, the proposed changes are realisable by all states, although the degree of difficulty will inevitably change from system to system.

Chapter V

About Political Parties

Wherever a group of people comes together with a common purpose, a common interest of that group (*organisational interest*) develops. This can be a company, sports club, group of friends, religious community or any other organisation. A company's organisational interest, for example, is to generate profits. A religious community seeks to share their spiritual journey. As long as organisational interests do not inflict harm on anyone, nothing will speak against any group pursuing their interests. The same holds true for all organisations, with one exception. One form of organisation is structurally dangerous, namely political parties.

Political parties are a social invention that aims to make public representation in political governments more efficient. Because there are many dissimilar groups within a society, a political party's goal is to represent the people of such a group in government. One defining factor, for example, can be income. Workers, who are usually economically weaker, have, in general, different perspectives on and expectations of their government's policy outputs. It is believed that the subgroups of a society can more effectively pursue their interests in government and push for favourable policy outputs through political parties. However, it would be foolish to assume that we can take shortcuts in matters of the state by implementing such mechanisms. The most obvious shortcoming of political parties is that they reduce the number of voices and nuanced approaches to a few mainstream sets of norms and values. Over time, our perception of politics is gradually reduced to the available parties – our thinking becomes limited. This is because parties can assert political prominence, due to better organisation and funding, compared to individual politicians. Accordingly, our views of what is politically thinkable is limited to the available parties as parties create thought monopolies. Further, parties will also develop organisational interests. Since these interests are structured around the common but one-dimensional theme of the party, the interests cannot be fully aligned with the objective interest of the whole society, although parties claim that they do so. It is logically impossible. The societal interests are undividable. It follows that, in theory, only one party could be the true defender of the societal interests. However, because they are born from the desire to represent one specific subgroup of the society, no party really works for the societal interest but for the interests of this subgroup.[15] To gain political power, they will have to influence

---

[15] It must also be noted that other risk factors are present here as well. Power structures of political parties are often not strictly regulated, and staffing is mostly left unscrutinised. It follows that there are a number of potential inefficiencies within political parties that amplify their negative policy performance.

the public opinion in a way that convinces the majority of the population that their party truly defends the societal interests. Over this factor, parties also tend to move away from technocratic policymaking or even tend to develop radical tendencies.

It is hard to sustain that a government's policy production can be structured around one or two guiding principles while remaining effective and efficient over a longer period. Hence, parties inherently limit our available policy options because they structure their whole approach to politics around a few guiding themes and compete with other parties with contradicting themes over power. Gaining power within a state then becomes a matter of ideology and pride, neglecting the objective interest of the society and hampering genuine knowledge production. Politics is not a matter of opinion or ideology. The only normative principle that should guide politicians' behaviour is their attachment to the good of the society. While every politician would claim to have such an attachment, the only behavioural pattern that truly displays this desire to elevate the own society is the technocratic approach to enable genuine knowledge production. Because it is the purpose of our existence, one can only be convinced of the good intentions of a politician if she enables or supports us to fulfil our purpose. Therefore, the same group of politicians can implement two very different courses of policy actions at different times without it being a behavioural incoherence. For example, politicians can raise taxes at one point in time and lower these very same taxes for the same or different reasons if such a move makes sense from a technocratic point of view. Political parties do not allow such a thing to happen as there are policy courses they would categorically exclude and categorically resort to. For example, a conservative party would not favour an expansive welfare programme, while a socialist party would not support the abolition of free healthcare.

Devletist systems do not allow for political parties. In fact, devletist systems do not allow any other organisation to exist that claims to defend the society's interests on the political level. Eventually, every such group will develop distinct organisational interests which are incoherent with the objective interest of the society.

The military is an exemption. It is the only organisation that should retain a semi-independent status from the state because it is the guardian of the nation and has intervention rights in case the state moves too far away from working on the improvement of the society to achieve genuine knowledge production. Even so, the military only has exceptional intervention powers and shall not interfere with regular government business. Furthermore, since the organisational interest of the military is clearly defined and aligned with the purpose of the state, it does not pose a threat to a state's proper functioning, which political parties do.

Chapter VI

The Devletist Voting System

Inherently linked to the idea that there should not be any political parties within any political system, we need a different mode of representation of the society within the government. Earlier, it was asserted that any form of rule (one person, a few selected persons or the whole society) can be of devletist nature. Today, we might be inclined to think that monarchies and aristocracies are less capable of representing the society due to the comprehensive powers of the ruler or rulers. However, since devletist systems are designed to enhance genuine knowledge production, monarchies and aristocracies, too, are bound to represent the societal interest. Throughout history, monarchs have frequently claimed to be doing just that, but their actions seldom followed their words. Especially in medieval Europe, there were prolonged phases of stagnation in genuine knowledge production while rulers claimed to be acting in accordance with national interests. [16] Because of the experience with those forms of rule moving away from societal interest, we are inclined to think that these two forms of rule are incapable of representing

---

[16] It is widely held that the arbitrary behaviour of monarchs in France, Spain, the fragmented German territories and England widely led to poor policy results, which, in turn, led to popular dissatisfaction.

societal interest. In theory, a devletist monarchy or devletist aristocracy can fulfil the state's purpose just as well. But in practise, it is certainly more difficult since the ease at which powers could potentially be misused contrasts with the greater difficulties rulers in devletist democracies would face if they were to further their personal interests instead of societal interests.[17]

Nonetheless, this is, unfortunately, happening in contemporary democracies, where rulers and political parties claim to be truly representing societal interests while, in reality, furthering personal or organisational interests. In any form of government, the ruling side will always try to legitimise its own rule through the consent of the people – even when it is vested with absolute powers. Naturally, the rulers of any political system, including most high-ranking officials, will have a cognitive advantage over the vast majority of people, paired with significant material means to influence the masses, which means they will have the ability to manipulate popular opinion. This can be during an election or in the wake of important political decisions. No ruling class can ever sustain their political course over an extended period without popular consent. This is inherently grounded in

---

[17] It goes without saying that devletist monarchies and oligarchies would be equipped with suitable structures to minimise such a misuse. In contrast to the diffused power within devletist democracies, however, the other forms of rule are better positioned to misuse power due to the concentrated form of their power.

the nature of government which is to administer the population. The farther away the underlying interests of a political course of action is from the objective societal interest, the greater the resistance by the people (given that the population is somewhat conscious of their interests). And hence, the greater the need of such rulers to manipulate popular opinion.

What follows is that any political system needs to ensure that the ruling class of a nation acts in the interest of the society, which is to create an environment for effective and efficient advancement of genuine knowledge production. By removing political parties, Devletism addresses one of the biggest shortcomings of contemporary political systems. A second obstacle that hinders the goal-oriented composition of a government is the mode by which the rulers of a nation receive their powers. In democratic systems, this is the voting system.

Before we dive into the structural specifics of the voting system, it is important to explore some underlying notions first. There are a couple of requirements a voting system needs to fulfil. First, it needs to ensure that the rulers, who are vested with the powers to govern the nation, act in accordance with the purpose of the state. This means that the system also needs to ensure that the rulers cannot misuse these powers to further their personal interest, in whatever form they might come. Second, and closely linked to the previous point, in the process of being vested with those powers, the candidates shall not have the opportunity to manipulate public opinion, in order to get elected or selected. These structural weaknesses can be addressed by a strong state. A strong state structure is one that does not rely on the individuals its government is composed of, meaning that the societal advancement through policy outputs is not linked to the level of individual talent of the President, Prime Minister or any other high-ranking civil servant – although the quality of advancement is influenced by them to a certain degree. If that is not the case, a system is bound to rise and fall with the quality of the rulers, which devletist systems aim to prevent. The devletist state structure ensures that societal advancement is given at any time, though the pace and quality is influenced by the aggregate quality of all individuals and the quality of their policy output.[18] In contrast to other systems, the reduction of the systemic downside risk of detrimental policy output is explicitly tackled through all stages of a truly devletist state, limiting the potential decrease in policy performance through human error. Especially, in the long run, devletist systems nearly erase the risk of stagnation, decline or systemic failure.

The technocratic character of bureaucracies needs to stretch all the way up to the highest ranks of a state. Within such an order,

---

[18] We cannot realistically expect that nations continuously operate at their peak performance rate, though this must unquestionably be the bar against which we should measure policy performance. Nations can compensate for periods of slight underperformance if they remain close to the ideal development rate. Naturally, occurring overperformance periods will make up for lost societal progress.

the high posts within a government lose much of their attractiveness in terms of egocentric considerations. In other words, a devletist system does not allow people to long for positions within the government to fulfil their personal desires for power. Rather, filling such a post should be considered a burden for the politicians. They are servants of the state, nation and, ultimately, society and, thus, are forced to channel their whole energy into fulfilling the purpose of all three of them. Within a devletist state, there is no room for dramatic speeches, exaggerations, loud discussions or anything that is linked to radical emotions. A devletist state must strive to embody the highest level of rational organisational productivity – and so must devletist politicians.

Due to lack of historical examples, with the European Union being the closest to a devletist system, it is difficult to detach politics from these aforementioned weaknesses. Especially, voting procedures are prone to be misused by politicians who long for power and glory. A suitable way to filter out these people while maintaining public representation is to tie political posts to minimum requirements. Just as all other government positions require applicants to fulfil a minimum degree of qualifications, ministers and presidents, as well as emperors, queens, kings, consuls and aristocrats, need to fulfil specific requirements, too. These should lay unproportionally above the educational average of the population and should, in general, be extremely hard to meet for any individual. For example, a president should perfectly master at least two foreign languages next to the official languages of the nation. Further, a strong academic background in the political sciences is indispensable. Ideally, all ministers and presidents should at least have a doctoral or even postdoctoral degree in the political sciences, along with a successful track record within national or international politics. Of course, there are many other things to consider, but the idea is that there need to be highly ambitious criteria to be fulfilled as politics is a serious matter. Only in that way the government can ensure that a certain quality standard is sustained. And only by doing that we can already reduce the probability of candidates relying solely on their rhetoric and organisational abilities to manipulate public opinion in their favour and gain power within the state.

However, this alone is not sufficient. The terms of ministers and presidents must be limited to reasonable time frames. This produces enough pressure on politicians to achieve significant advancements for the nation but also ensures they will not become bigger than the system they are working for.

Another structural aspect is the mode of election. It should be clear that every individual makes most of her decisions based on a certain degree of information that she has access to. Never are we making decisions randomly with the expectation of a high-quality result. Rather, we want to have the maximum amount of accessible, relevant information before we make any decision.

The amount of information that flows into our decisions significantly determines the quality of the outcomes. Because the outcomes of voting decisions are of unmatched importance to any nation's development, we need to take this into consideration when designing our voting system. Traditionally, every person has one vote in democratic elections. These may be local, provincial, national or supranational elections. Usually, the only voting requirement that exists is that voters need to reach a certain age before being eligible to cast a vote. However, the age of a person alone does not influence the amount and quality of information that a person has on a certain topic – both amount and quality of information on politics is relevant to make sane voting decisions. Furthermore, with the universal right to vote, the importance of each vote is the same, undermining high-quality voting decisions by people with a heightened understanding of politics. Moreover, it also creates the misconception that voting is a natural right. Just as any other decision is a process of consciousness and proactivity and, thus, requires a certain thought process to take place beforehand, voting decisions, all the more, require a proactive confrontation with the subject matter, as the nation's future development is inherently linked to those decisions. Instead of viewing the participation in the voting process as a right, it must rather be viewed as a qualification that needs to be obtained. This is another important assumption within the devletist school of thought: political participation is not a naturally granted right but rather a qualification that needs to be obtained through genuinely interacting with the subject matter of politics. How can a society expect their politicians to fulfil minimum requirements when they themselves are indifferent to the political dealings of the state? How can one without an interest in the development of the nation have the right to decide on the fate of this very nation?

The solution is to introduce an examination scheme that enables citizens to obtain votes for elections of politicians. There should be ten stages that correlate with a maximum of ten votes a citizen can obtain. After passing the first exam, a citizen is qualified to cast one vote and is granted the right to also enter the second examination stage and so on. This first exam will, naturally, be the easiest stage, asking the citizens simple questions, such as the location of the nation on the world map, date of establishment, name of the capital and other fundamental aspects related to national politics and politics in general. It must be argued that a person who does not know these simple things about the nation and politics is not interested in the development of the nation as well. If one is not interested in the development of her nation, then she must not have a say in who is going to rule the nation through the state – let alone be given the same amount of voting power as citizens who are interested in the nation's development.

The degree of difficulty of the exams increases with every stage, while the tenth level, granting ten votes if passed, will ask participants to answer highly complex questions that require an incredible amount of technical knowledge of politics and society; every minister and president should constantly pass this tenth level. While the exams can be taken every month – with a six month ban after three consecutive unsuccessful tries – in order to be able to add more voting power to one's name, each year, people will be downgraded one level, and two levels after every national election. Doing so ensures that the citizens of the nation are constantly pressured to improve themselves. Voting power then becomes a matter of constant engagement with the political system and politics of such a devletist system will reinforce its focus on technocratic governing.

Pairing the minimum requirements of politicians with the voting system, which grants knowledgeable citizens more voting powers than indifferent citizens, the staffing of government posts ensures a high degree of technocratic standards within the government. Further, there is a certain depolitisation that will develop with such a voting system. Personal considerations of prestige, fame and pride are significantly overshadowed by the need to be a master of (politician) and expert on (citizen) statecraft. People who embark on the endeavour to become a technocratic mastermind will surely be able to identify more suitable politicians when they cross their ways. Instead of competing against those more suitable people, a technocratic mastermind will assist those others with her expertise, since this is more useful for the nation as a whole.[19] The ones who are unfamiliar with the depths of political technicalities will always put their personal thirst for fame over the state's need to create an environment of effective and efficient production of genuine knowledge for its society. Those people must be prevented from entering the government.

---

[19] Even if politicians are competitive, the devletist system only allows them to exceed the next person through cognitive advancement. This is only conducive for the nation. In contemporary political systems, politicians mostly compete through manipulation of popular opinion.

Chapter VII

About Governance

The specifics of a government are always tied to the societal characteristics of a nation. Within ethnically homogeneous societies, federal structures are thinkable as the risk of separatist tendencies is lower, compared to heterogeneous societies. However, it also depends on whether the ethnic heterogeneity is concentrated geographically or is mixed throughout the territory of the nation. If a society is heterogeneous, but all territories display a relatively balanced ethnic composition of the local population, federal systems might work as well. It also depends on whether the ethnic differences are big or small and whether they are balanced by a strong common national identity. Generally, heterogeneous societies, such as the society of the Turkish Republic, should be governed centrally. Nonetheless, every state should have three levels of governance, with an optional fourth level, depending on the societal composition and intersocietal proximity to other nations.

There should be a local governance level entrusted with developing and implementing policies at the city level. Here, policies which are decided upon at the national level are implemented, but also policies according to the local needs are required to be developed within the range of the competences received from the central government. Urban planning is one of the core exclusive competences of local politics. Of course, it must adhere to the legal frame set out by the central government, but the implementation needs to primarily address local circumstances, which is why it is a matter of local governance. Also, the local authorities must predominantly shape the local economy. A city within the mountains has different infrastructural needs, advantages and possibilities than a city at the seaside. In this example, the central government must determine which cities at a coastline might be more suitable for the development of tourism or trade, while local politics is entrusted with the specific design of the local economy. Is the development of domestic tourism or international tourism more suitable? Is the trade primarily based on manufactured goods or on raw materials, which will require different logistical infrastructures? All this needs consideration.

The actor who is some sort of mediator between the central/national government and the local government is the provincial government. It puts the individual management of the local constituencies into the context of the broader region of the province. It needs to ensure that provincial politics does not become one-sided, meaning there should be a socio-economic harmony within the province. For example, mountainous provinces might face procurement challenges in terms of resources. To reduce transaction costs, the province must be managed in a way that the geographical advantages of each city are used and connected with one another. Further, risk management must be coordinated through provincial governance. Coast guards, police forces and medical infrastructures should enable efficient, coordinated action within a province to ensure swift responses when a city's resources are insufficient to cope with unforeseen circumstances by itself. The role of provincial governments in federal systems is much greater. Here, they are called federal governments and also set the direction in policy areas, such as education or even taxation, depending on the competences it receives through the political system.[20] In central governments, provincial governments have a strongly communicative and organisational role.[21] They voice the aggregated local needs, which become the provincial needs, to the central government and design the general course of development within the province according to the strategy of the central government. The mutual dialogue between central and provincial governments helps to identify geographical and demographic needs, advantages and disadvantages of certain regions within a nation. Accordingly, the central government can

---

[20] In Germany, the federal governments have far-reaching competences in matters of education, whereas, in Canada, the provincial governments can set individual tax rates for their respective province.

[21] Implementation of central government orders can be seen as communicative. Depending on the system, however, provincial governments retain some sort of flexibility in their policymaking, especially in policy areas that require adaptation to provincial circumstances.

coordinate and harmonise them with other provinces. The dialogue between provincial and local governments is important to monitor the implementation of the central government's strategy but also for the local government to communicate local needs and proposals for further development.

Then there is the central government. It is the mastermind behind any nation's course of development. The central government needs to identify the nation's geographical specifics and what advantages and disadvantages come with them. Climate, resources, location, neighbouring states and their politics, amount of renewable water resources and risk of disasters are only a handful among many more factors that need consideration at this level. Further, the demographic characteristics need to be identified, too. Age, geographical distribution, common health issues, nutritional tendencies, mentality, history, religious and ethnic composition and many other characteristics need to be clearly identified, constantly monitored, updated and evaluated. With this geographic and demographic knowledge about the nation, a central government needs to formulate policy outputs within feasible strategies that help all citizens to engage in genuine knowledge production. These strategies are subject to constant change and needs to be adapted in ways that ensure a highly effective approach to societal progress. The core aspects of such a strategy are the proper design of the education system, economic structure and policy, foreign policy and military, urban planning and infrastructure, welfare system and the judiciary.[22] Obviously, with changing geographic and demographic situations, the strategy of the central government should also change, though not as radical as one might think since the adaptation process is incremental. As mentioned earlier, the dialogue between the provincial and local governments helps to understand the specifics of those governance levels better, and the central government can shape its approaches accordingly.

At the very beginning of this chapter, it was indicated that there is an optional fourth level of governance. This is the supranational level and could potentially become the most important level of governance within the next four to five centuries. The supranational level of governance is the level at which states among themselves make authoritative and binding decisions that need to be implemented throughout all nations which are unified under the supranational government. It exceeds national boundaries and harmonises those policy areas currently subject to the lowest level of popular polarisation, such as production standards or traffic rules. However, at later stages of supranational integration, legislative, judicative and executive authority over more and more policy areas can be delegated to

---

[22] These are the six policy areas that will be dealt with in greater detail in the second part of this work.

the supranational government. In theory, a supranational structure could become to the national governance level, what the national governance level is currently to the provincial governance level. While current supranational structures' development is strongly hampered by emotional considerations of national governments, devletist supranational entities are fully technocratic and, therefore, able to harmonise all policy areas and set the most suitable strategy within them.

The main purpose of the supranational governance level is to increase policy efficiency by bundling national resources and achieving an effective and efficient environment for genuine knowledge production over a much greater territory. Further, a vast majority of transaction costs is saved as economic and legal conduct between the nations is not subject to customs, duties, fees or the work of intermediaries. Another great advantage is that the supranational bloc has a much stronger military force, which radically increases all member nations' chances of survival. The increased economic power will allow the bloc to advance more quickly due to more and better political and economic tools. However, an important prerequisite for establishing effective supranational structures is that the member nations are ethnically and culturally highly similar. For example, the European Union is the biggest and most well-functioning supranational entity in history. The reason for that is that the integration process of the member nations was born out of a common cultural understanding, which, in turn, stems from many nations' similar ethnic properties. Of course, on the surface, the political considerations drove the European nations to adopt measures that ultimately led to the establishment of the European Union. However, the fact that it is functioning so effectively is grounded in the reality that the cultural understanding among the nations is highly cohesive, although this is often perceived differently. China, for example, would not be able to establish a supranational bloc with other nations because there are no other ethnicities that are culturally or ethnically close to the Chinese people. However, Latin American, North African, Arab, Slavic and Turkic nations are more than suitable for establishing large supranational systems that would foster growth and development among their member nations.

Chapter VIII

Electing Local, Provincial and Central Government Officials

Now, that we have explored the specifics of the voting system as well as the different levels of governance, we can combine those two elements and restructure the mode of societal representation in the government around the principles outlined above. Albeit referenda are less likely to produce inefficient outcomes in devletist systems because of their weighted voting system based on political knowledge, they are not desirable. Citizens cannot, and should not, spend their time exclusively engaging in the political system. Basing politics on referenda would require citizens to use all their energy on research and analysis of the subject matters at hand, next to an already increased contact with political matters, due to the voting system. This would prevent citizens from pursuing their professions or at least would severely hamper the quality of their work, which would be counterproductive to the aim of genuine knowledge production.

Hence, the citizens should mandate their sovereignty and be represented by politicians. The voting system not only ensures that the most knowledgeable citizens can cast more votes and, thus, increase the chances of electing the most suitable politicians, but the minimum requirements that politicians need to fulfil further decrease the margin of error by setting minimum standards for politicians within the devletist system. With the removal of parties from the political system, the focus will be completely directed toward the candidates' skills, and because of that, the need for election campaigns will also be removed. We will later see that other factors of personal campaigning will be accounted for. In a system with an increased minimum understanding of political processes, paired with a greater focus on societal advancement, there is no need to convince voters with slogans and promises. Also, this wastes considerable time and resources while leading to goal displacement. Politics is not a playground for egocentric people who solely want their names to be printed in history books. Just like any other aspect within a devletist political environment, elections are a matter of technicalities.

Beginning with local elections, representatives should be elected for a term of two to four years, which can only be renewed once. Local politics is much more fast-paced, and developments are more visible and tangible. Accordingly, politicians need to be put under pressure to achieve notable progress. Over time, this will also raise the level of expectation on the side of the citizens because they will naturally expect that the local representative and her cadre produce meaningful policy outputs during their time in office, whereas prolonged terms in office remove the urgency of efficient policymaking. The quality will not suffer under such short terms because the devletist structure already removed the greatest barriers to political efficiency by filtering out unsuitable candidates and removing the ideology factor through the abolition of parties. These factors create the greatest friction at all policy levels as political discourse becomes tied to personal beliefs, and this emotional discussion hampers a technical dialogue.

The election process starts with the need for an election. A politician's term ends, she retires by wish, is removed from office and so on. A government institution is then entrusted with the review of the candidate requirements. The institution reviews the requirements based on whether they reflect the current development status of the nation. Here, it is important that there should never be a downside correction of the requirements for political candidates. It must be a central institution, and the requirements for local representatives and their cadres need to be applied to all local constituencies, in order to achieve even development throughout the nation. In addition to those tasks, this institution is also responsible for the composition of the examinations through which votes are obtained. Further, this institution – we shall call it the election ministry – needs to have offices within the local government in order to administer local voting exams, process applications and coordinate the campaigns of the candidates. Once the requirements are set, the election ministry receives the applications locally. Every citizen who fulfils the formal requirements to run for the post of the local representative needs to be admitted.[23] It is every citizen's natural right within a democratic political system to have the chance to run for a post, given that she unambiguously fulfils the requirements. In cases where there is ambiguity or even wilful wrongdoing or fraud, the highest court of the state should rule on these matters.

In the application process, there should be at least five candidates running for the post. In exceptionally small constituencies, there might be a shortage of qualified people to fill the post. Here, the election ministry can turn to a database of all current and former applicants across the nation and invite them to run for this specific post. If this is also insufficient to let at least five people run for election, the ministry can actively source for people who might fulfil the requirements and invite them to run for election. If this does not bring the number of candidates to five either, an election with at least three people can be held. In the very few cases where not even three candidates can be found, the term of the reigning local representative is prolonged by a half-term, and if the problem persists at the next election, the local constituency is merged with the closest suitable local constituency. It means that this locality is incapable of producing sufficient qualified and motivated people, which neutralises its right to own local governance. Since the sole aim

---

[23] The same also applies to all political elections.

of Devletism is to push for collective progress through knowledge production, the inability to raise suitable politicians is a clear indicator of failed policymaking. Needless to say, this should seldom be the case.

After identifying a pool of suitable candidates, the campaigning process begins. It should only last a period of four weeks and must be subject to strict control and supervision by the election ministry. The difference between election campaigning in devletist systems and contemporary democratic systems is that elections in the former are administered by the government. Most importantly, the communication between the broader public and the candidates must run through official channels. Therefore, the election ministry plays a crucial role here, too. It organises televised and openly accessible panel discussions between the candidates as well as structured individual speeches by the candidates. It is also responsible for summarising the candidates' resumes and formulating their policy programmes in standardised forms while also responsible for distributing this information to the public online and in paper form, where needed. Finally, the election ministry supervises the actual election by organising the election venues, counting the votes and announcing the outcome. With regard to the election venues, it is suitable that citizens cast their votes in schools, which has a very symbolic character in the light of the devletist ideal of a knowledge-oriented society where education is the central aspect of the nation.

Now that we have explored the election process of local representatives, we can turn to the next level of governance, the provincial level. Within central systems, there is no need to elect representatives in the provincial government. Because the provincial government is entrusted with mainly organisational, structural and communicative tasks within centralised political systems, it is sufficient that the provincial parliament, consisting of all local representatives from the province, elects a provincial "Prime Minister" among themselves to lead the dealings of the province. For federal systems, the situation is much different. Here, provincial governments are vested with far-reaching competences that sometimes even include legislative powers in matters of education, taxation or other policy fields. In such systems, the same election procedure, which applies to the local elections, should be applied here to elect provincial representatives, with the exception that their terms in office should range between three to five years as provincial policies due to their increased complexity, take more time in terms of implementation and unfolding their effects. The minimum criteria for provincial representatives in federal systems shall be more ambitious in comparison to those applied to local representatives. This is not only applied to the election of provincial officials to the provincial parliament in federal systems but also an additional level of the election of provincial officials in centralised systems. Here, representatives are elected at the provincial level but for representative functions in the national parliament. According to the size of the provinces, seats within the national parliament are allocated. To fill those seats, the citizens elect candidates from their province to represent the provincial population at the national level. The requirements for those people are naturally even more ambitious than those for the local representatives. Furthermore, they will also have terms between four to five years long, again, with a one-time renewal chance. These provincial representatives are not involved in the provincial parliament's (composed of the local representatives of the nation) workings, though they do need to stay in close contact with each other since they have a representative function and need to be informed about the provincial developments.[24] The main function of those representatives is policymaking together with the head of government at the national level. Therefore, they need to be highly skilled as they are the main actors in the policy process.

In any system, the most important election is the national election. Again, the same procedure from the local election is generally applied here, though with a couple of modifications.

---

[24] They are members of the national parliament, elected by the provincial population. The provincial parliament is composed of the elected local representatives.

First, the terms for the office of the Head of Government shall be between four to five years, being subject to one renewal. The logic remains the same: with increased population and territory to govern, politics becomes more complex, and policies require significantly more time to unfold their effects. However, because we do not want people to become bigger than the system they operate in, the position of the Head of Government needs to be renewed frequently. This leads to the next aspect, which is concerned with the candidate requirements. If the same academic and professional requirements that are asked of candidates for the post of a local representative are also asked of candidates who run for the position of the Head of Government, then the number of applications would be overwhelming. This would make it impossible for citizens to make sound voting decisions, due to the overload of options. Also, the Head of Government has significantly more powers and responsibilities than politicians at the lower levels of governance. It follows that the Head of Government must be considerably more skilled, knowledgeable and experienced than the politicians at those lower levels of governance. Ideally, the Head of Governance embodies the pinnacle of human development in every aspect of life.[25] In the end, she does not only decide on the fate of millions of citizens

---

[25] As this office is the most important in any nation, expecting perfection from the incumbent is unquestionably reasonable.

but also represents the nation in the world and functions as a role model for every citizen. Hence, the candidate's requirements for the role of the Head of Government need to be extremely ambitious. Ideally, in the course of every election, the process will bring forward five to twenty candidates who meet the requirements. At this point, the election as an act of voting would become merely a matter of nuances. All the candidates would be capable of governing the nation, but they will have slightly stronger or weaker points in different disciplines compared to the other candidates.

Once a candidate is elected, she will appoint her ministers and seek approval of her appointees from the national parliament through a two-third majority, once a ministerial post is to be filled. Every minister has a three-year term but can be reappointed five times, so that a minister can serve a maximum of fifteen years. Here, it is important to have longer terms as the ministers provide a form of continuity within the political system. They should be specialised and highly familiar with the ministry's subject matter and its organisational history.[26] Moreover, the political system also needs to be shielded from nepotism. If the cadre of ministers changes with every election,

---

[26] We can observe in many contemporary systems that ministers try to switch to ministries they perceive to be more prestigious, raising questions whether ministries are merely steps on the career ladder for them. In such cases, ministries tend to underperform.

it can be reasonably assumed that the Head of Government is trying to appoint people close to her thinking or even people whom she has personal ties. Another mechanism that prevents Heads of Governments from doing so, is that, here again, the Election Ministry sets minimum requirements for the ministerial posts, which lay, in terms of ambitiousness, between the level of the Members of the Parliament and the Head of Government. Further, any citizen who fulfils the requirements for this post can file an application to the Election Ministry at any time, and if they decide that the criteria are met (which needs to be a transparent and openly accessible procedure), the candidate or candidates will be put to a parliamentary vote, next to the appointee of the Head of Government and the current holder of the office, the next time the specific ministerial position is to be filled.

With such extended powers, and basically the fate of the nation laying in its hands, the Election Ministry has somewhat a special role within the government. While its policymaking is significantly limited to its core tasks, the quality of the functioning of the ministry is crucial in determining the overall quality of the political system. Accordingly, it needs to be subject to control mechanisms as well as retaining a sufficient amount of independence. This ministry, unlike other ministries, should be governed through a council of eleven to twenty-one highly-skilled people. They should be subject to the same requirements as the regular ministers and be selected by the parliament for a term of ten to fifteen years, which is non-renewable. The reason being that they need to outlive much of the political cadre's terms, in order to become detached from their intragovernmental competition but also remain motivated enough to deliver as much quality output as possible within their single term. Furthermore, their selection by the parliament needs to be put to popular vote from the citizens. As a ministry practically embodying the core ideas of democratic policymaking, citizens must be able to approve or veto the appointees. This election does not reset any voting rights, as the purpose of this vote is merely to provide a balancing mechanism against the selection powers of the parliament.

Chapter IX

The Devletist Parliament

Although we have explored the composition of the parliament and the election procedure of its members in quite some detail, its functioning needs to be looked at in greater detail. With the removal of parties, the parliament ceases to be a showroom of battles for ideological and rhetorical high ground. The core principle of the parliament remains the same: it represents the society within the state and forms the central body of policymaking within the government. Its members are, as mentioned earlier, subject to minimum requirements to be eligible to stand for election. These also need to be comparatively ambitious requirements. However, the functioning of the parliament under Devletism is different.

A devletist parliament is structured like a moderated discussion forum, which is the heart of the legislative. The Head of Government acts as the moderator of discussions on the agenda. The agenda, in turn, will be voted on in the parliament after taking suggestions from its members. For example, at the end of every parliamentary session, points of discussion are raised by the members and will be placed on the agenda for the session 30 days after the vote. It should be noted that the agendas should leave enough room for urgent matters or important topics that come up unexpectedly. In case of more important topics or unexpected events and emergencies, extraordinary sessions of the parliament shall be arranged by the office of the Head of Government itself or on the demand of the qualified majority (two-thirds) of the members of the parliament, directed to the office of the Head of Government.

A typical discussion would start with an opening statement by the Head of Government and an oath that everything in the parliament shall be done in the interest of the nation. Then the agenda points of the day are listed and can be altered if the parliament deems this necessary. Once the procedure starts, the Head of Government presents the topic at hand, explains the problem, legal considerations tied to it, states priorities in solving the issue and proposes a possible policy response. All these are based on the analyses and evaluations of the Head of Government's office and other sources of research and merely have the legal status of a recommendation. This, however, is an important aspect since it provides the members of the parliament with a general overview and a first reliable point of reference. Of course, since the agendas are public long before the session, the members of the parliament, supported by their respective offices, are expected to be well prepared for each session.

In the next step, the aim of the discussion is to reach a broad consensus, effectively agreeing on a general direction and then narrowing it down to a specific goal. Therefore, the Head of

Government moderates a discussion within the parliament on what the desired result might look like. It is important that the Head of Government balances the discussion in terms of talking time, filters out the most important points raised by the representatives, identifies potential problems and also keeps the discussion constructive and streamlined. Because ideological and personal financial interests are eliminated and the parliament is subject to public scrutiny, the discussions must be purely technical. The overarching principle, which guides all actions and inactions within every single corner of the state, is the goal of societal advancement through the process of genuine knowledge production.

Moving on from the discussion on the policy goals of a certain agenda point, the Head of Government also moderates the second part of the discussion, which is about the potential solutions to the problem which is effectively the search for an effective and efficient policy. Once there is a clearer view on the goals, problems and solutions to the topic at hand, the Head of Government asks for volunteers in the parliament to work out a draft legislation within an agreed period. If there are no volunteers, the Head of Government determines a team based on recommendations from the parliament. Then the parliament moves on to the next topic and repeats this procedure.

With regard to other aspects of the parliament, there must be a television channel as well as a radio channel and an online livestream which broadcast all the meetings of the parliament at full length and without comments. Also, these, or separate, channels shall broadcast the interviews of the candidates, elections and selection processes. In short, every person in the world should have direct and unhindered access to what is said in a devletist parliament. Furthermore, if citizens in remote areas do not have the chance to obtain access to those sources, they shall be provided with free transcripts of all the meetings in paper form upon their request. These citizens shall receive a list of adopted legislation with brief summaries at least biannually. Devletist systems aim to achieve maximum inclusion and engagement of the citizens. This is crucial in the light of the voting system, which requires citizens to engage in a continuous development process in terms of politics. If people cannot easily access all the information, the system will quickly favour those who can access relevant information more easily. Ideally, all people stay informed at all times, deeply engage with the matters of the nation and seek to further improve themselves in the realm of politics, next to their personal pursuit of genuine knowledge.

Chapter X

From Principles to Policymaking

Until now, we have explored the concept of Devletism, its philosophical underpinnings, key terms and important material structures of one version of a devletist state. While there are certainly many more aspects that could, and also ought to be, altered in contemporary political systems, they are less relevant to the core design of the state. For example, whether the reporting structure within a ministry is rather hierarchical or horizontal is a matter that influences the achievement of genuine knowledge production to a much lesser extent than implementing the voting system outlined earlier. Moreover, how policy areas are divided and put under the authority of ministries also does not influence our aim of genuine knowledge production to such an extent that an extensive discussion would be warranted within the scope of this work. It needs to be added that, gladly, these matters are already functioning at a high level of technocratic policymaking throughout most political systems. However, what is significantly more important than those administerial aspects of governance, are the subject matters of the distinct policy areas a state has legislative, executive and judicial powers over. Rather than restructuring the administrative processes within, for example, the Education Ministry, rethinking the core premises, principles and some structures of education policy would add more value to the understanding of how Devletism would approach policy matters, in order to increase the efficiency of genuine knowledge production.

Therefore, we will now turn to the respective policy areas. Though the material proposals were developed in the light of the state's purpose, they coexist with a wide range of other potential courses of policy actions, aligned with the devletist idea and possibly exceeding my humble approaches in effectiveness and efficiency to further genuine knowledge production within a society. In no way would I arrogate myself to portray proposals, discussed in this work, as blueprints of the perfect policy design. Rather, I hope they serve as inspirations for sympathisers of the devletist school, to develop much more sophisticated approaches to devletist policymaking. Again, the design of the material side of policymaking is heavily dependent on the cultural specifics of the nation they are applied to. A nation that is geographically well-suited to structuring its economy around the export of agricultural goods, for instance, will have an inherently different economic structure than a nation that relies heavily on the services sector or on manufacturing. These specifics, in turn, affect other policy areas, such as urban planning, education and foreign policy, as well. It follows that one limited universal approach cannot produce meaningful outcomes for more than one nation – if for any.

However, my humble attempts to form meaningful policy proposals, within the different policy areas, play a rather subordinate role within this part of this work. The primary focus is on the guiding principles which underlie policymaking within the specific policy areas. Considerations of what should be the aims within each policy area translate the abstract devletist ideals into clear formulations of policy guidelines, meaning that this part of the policy areas is much more tangible. Again, there are many different potential courses of policy action to reach those aims and also achieve those changes within the normative framework of Devletism. But without guidance, policymaking would quickly suffer from goal displacement. Therefore, it is inevitable that the perception of how a state should approach policy matters must not only be aligned with the purposes of the society and the state, but also needs to harmonise horizontally across the different policy areas. This is a holistic approach to policymaking and in contrast to the often independent development of different branches of politics, like we can observe in contemporary systems.

One example, that one can easily observe, is the increasing divergence between the development of education systems and economies. Over the last century, the structure of most economies is decreasingly rewarding academic brilliance, while increasingly favouring consumption-oriented economic behaviour both on the supply and demand sides of the economy, effectively harming the importance of the education system. Originally, education systems aimed at developing young talent to not only add to the various scientific fields but also to enhance the nation's prosperity through economic conduct. With the disproportionately high consumerist effects of globalisation and corporatism, scholars from many scientific fields, which are less demanded in the economy or inherently generate less monetary returns, become economically and even socially marginalised, although they might add significantly more to the realisation of the nation's purpose than purely commercially oriented people. From this example, it follows that the normative and technical underpinnings of the different policy areas need to be rectified – not only to avert tendencies of goal displacement but also to create a proactive agenda for politicians and related professionals to alter their behaviour accordingly.

Chapter XI

About Devletism and the Politics of Left and Right

The term technocracy and other related notions around technocratic governance have appeared at various points in this work, already. Since it is a central aspect to devletist thinking, it demands special attention and, hence, further explanation. In essence, a technocratic political system is centred around the idea that the most capable people should be the rulers of a nation. Further, they aim at rational policymaking to enable efficient political functioning of the system. Thus, it becomes clear that devletist systems fall under the umbrella of technocracies. Yet merely stating that governments should simply do what is best for the nation in the most efficient way is too vague to be effectively translated into action. No current, past or future politician would claim that she is not doing just that. No matter how unsuccessful or harmful a politician's course of action is to a nation, her subjective perception of her own actions and motives are positive. If a politician is not able to produce meaningful outcomes for the nation, the system's structure is usually to blame rather than the politician. Exceptionally gifted statesmen were able to elevate their nations through their talent and persona. But within a flawed system, the average political performance will massively lag behind the output a mediocre cadre of politicians would produce within a system grounded in a strong political structure. Technocracies try to address this problem. Thus, Devletism aims at building and sustaining structures that provide continued quality policy performance.

Now, one major shortcoming of technocracies is the inherently qualitative aspect of identifying what is best for the nation. Linked to that, crafting policies is an endeavour that is characterised by great uncertainties. Since we cannot, at this point of our evolution, surely identify the objective truth, goal setting and policymaking remain difficult. But, this also holds true for any other form of government, though in contrast to workings of other political systems, technocracies leave less room for emotions that would limit the range of policy options or create policy biases. Different systems utilise different logics to produce meaningful policy outputs. Party-based democracies structure politics around ideological guidelines. As discussed above, this is somewhat tied to the different interests of the many different sub-groups within a society but has also a spiritual character. Parties at the left spectrum of the political categorisation have the conviction that a nation's wealth should rather be distributed, aiming at a universally increased living standard, which naturally requires more state intervention. On the right side, the traditionalist notions of the natural laws guide much of the thinking, as it is believed that both economic and social conduct should be balanced out by the dynamics of action and reaction, implying an opposing stance towards state intervention. Devletist systems are not bound to these spiritual approaches as the devletist politician would approach policymaking with the central conviction that the state needs to fulfil the nation's purpose to move closer to the understanding of the objective truth.

It is in the nature of things that the objective truth cannot be approached one-sidedly, as the existence and non-existence of everything is essentially part of this objective truth. The mere fact that our societies developed dynamics which require thinking about wealth distribution and self-governance shows that they are both essential parts of policymaking. Devletism acknowledges this. However, it should not be viewed that Devletism is a centrist approach which tries to find a compromise between the political left and the political right. Compromises and hybrid solutions are often the biggest enemies of effective policymaking. Rather, Devletism tries to get rid of these categorisations altogether and aims at situation-based policymaking. In other words, this means that every item on the political agenda is treated individually, which also includes the utilisation of its unique historical context. It is of inconceivable importance that every political matter is analysed properly, in order to be able to craft tailored approaches to its resolution. The more extensive the analysis of the political problem, the more effective the policy response. Such a political analysis is composed of three main pillars: historical context, evidence and culture.

Chapter XII

Political Analysis

Regarding the pillars of political analysis, the historical context is of massive importance here. Most of the political problems that we face at a certain point in time are rooted in seemingly unimportant social, economic or political dynamics of the past. These may date back several centuries, looking unrelated to current problems at first sight. For example, the Second World War is often connected to the German nation's dissatisfaction with the material burdens and political isolation which it was hit by after the First World War.[27] From this, one would follow that burdening a nation could pave the way for great developmental problems and even larger conflicts in the future. However, we could put the developments in another context which stretches back to the founding days of the German Empire in 1871.

While many nations in Europe already internalised the idea of the nation state, Germany was late to transform its loosely organised confederation into an outright nation state.[28] As it is

---

[27] Most notably, John Maynard Keynes (*The Economic Consequences of the Peace*, 1919) saw great danger in burdening Germany too much, even before the Second World War.

[28] From a systemic perspective, we need to compare the unified German Empire of 1871 with the Kingdom of France (987), Kingdom of England (927), Kingdom of Portugal (1139) and Kingdom of Spain (1479). The Kingdom of Italy (1861) and the Austrian Empire (1804) were established much later, and unsurprisingly followed similar paths as Germany.

with any major societal change that is centred around identity the euphoric young German nation had much ground to make up to level its power position against other European nations, which were using the idea of the nation state to their advantages for some centuries already. With a fresh and heightened awareness of its national identity, paired with comparatively little political experience, the incompatibilities with other European powers, which were able to establish a more or less levelled playing field in terms of political power among themselves, rose by the day. The developmental discrepancy in terms of national identity between Germany and the rest of the European powers became so great that the political balance could no longer be upheld. Not only did this German self-discovery process cause two large-scale wars but also left the nation divided for almost half a century in the aftermath of the war. The effects stretch all the way to contemporary German policymaking. The nation suffers from a great identity problem as the last thirty years were the only years the nation was truly stable and fully unified since the First World War. Further, with the heavy influence of the European Union, the process of solidifying a distinct German identity remains a difficult task.

Without this context, political analysis of German politics, in matters related to the outlined issue, is useless. There are countless examples of historical developments that current developments are rooted in. Another example is the *Monroe*

Doctrine of the United States of America as a central cause of the nation's rise to an unprecedented economic, military and cultural superpower.[29] We could also look at the benevolent social policies of the Ottoman Empire in the Arabic territories, which were rather administered than outright governed. In the later course of history, this caused the decay of much of the Arab world today. The time horizons which political analysts and politicians apply to analyse societal and political developments fall mostly short to encompass the complexity of an issue, which, paradoxically, is often grounded in quite simple developments in the past. It is useful to think about the historical context in terms of the life cycles of organisms. While we are often limited in our thinking to our own lifespan, or to only a few generations after us, the life cycles of civilisations stretch over significantly greater time frames and, therefore, developments need to be analysed in the light of those cycles. Devletists shed light on those issues from far greater angles, stressing the unimportance of individuals within the process of policymaking in the devletist school once again. Just as those past dynamics influence our current political and societal situations, our present actions will have

---

[29] The doctrine articulated a foreign policy that aimed to shield Latin America from European intervention and influences. Because European generally respected this doctrine, the United States of America themselves were able to exert exclusive influence on Latin American states. Through this mode of exclusive exploitation, the United States of America managed to amplify their economic output and already export their culture to Latin America during the 19th century.

repercussions in many centuries to come. With such an awareness, it would be more than foolish to expect that efficient and lasting progress can be achieved through the works of individuals. Historical context is, thus, a central element in the understanding of politics which, in turn, is essential to shape effective technocratic policies to enable, restore or improve genuine knowledge production.

The second central pillar of political analysis is the evidence-based approach to understanding societal and political events, phenomena and dynamics. Certainly, there is a connection to the historical dimension because the more data is available over a long period on a certain topic, the more effective political analysis can become. Yet, while the historical context is rather a more qualitative endeavour to make sense of societal and political dynamics, evidence-based political analysis seeks to quantify the understanding around the relevant topics to a certain extent. Naturally, this is much easier in policy areas such as the economy and urban planning than in areas such as education or the judiciary. Nonetheless, the collection of data and the methodological connection of vast amounts of datasets to identify correlations, with the aim to identify causations, is a central task of political scientists. With increasing data and the proper linking of the datasets, policymaking will become more efficient by the day. For example, the more we can find out about how the architecture of cities influence the productivity of the work force, mediated through the effects of quality of life, the better urban planning can be organised to boost economic output, while increasing personal well-being. Although these are seemingly unrelated parts of politics, there might be a significant connection that only large amounts of data and sound methodological approaches to their evaluation can validate or invalidate. Under the devletist logic, the aim is to remove as much uncertainty within the policymaking process as possible. Surely, other political systems aim to do the same, however, they are often hindered by the ideological boundaries of parties, interest groups or egocentric rulers. An example of such a situation would be the analysis of the effects of immigration on a society. Under the established normative framework of the United Nations antagonistic stances towards the topic of immigration are avoided as they directly conflict with the inclusive approach the United Nations wants to solidify, which is somewhat representative of the global approach to humanitarian politics of the day.[30] However, a devletist approach would not shy away from analysing any issue from all thinkable perspectives, even though it might appear counterintuitive to do so in the light of some normative frameworks. While ideological camps would have a pre-defined set of answers to questions around nearly all

---

[30] A representative example of this stance is the *Global Compact for Migration* (2018). Though it is of non-binding nature, it formulates a positive and protective normative framework for migration.

topics, Devletism does not rush to stigmatise courses of policy action. Interestingly, the outcome of the evidence-based analysis is totally irrelevant from an emotional perspective as the goal is to form effective and efficient policies in light of genuine knowledge production and not personal ideological preferences. Because the outcome of such an analysis can be different at two different points in time, stigmatising certain policy directions would lead to inefficiencies in policymaking.

However, the conclusions drawn from the evidence-based analysis alone might also lead to flawed policymaking without the historical context. Let us assume that the result of the evidence-based analysis on immigration shows that it, when from a certain nation, led to an increase in economic performance and the integration of those immigrants into society happened smoothly. One would be inclined to follow from this piece of information that a policy course which fosters further immigration from the said nation is in the interest of the own nation. However, if the own society has a history of separatism, is highly homogeneous or has a weak national identity, the positive findings from the evidence-based analysis could have negative effects when we put them in the light of the historical context.[31] The combination of higher economic performance of

---

[31] We can think about historical context also in the future since the long-term developments, though naturally unknown in the present, can be much different than results obtained in the short- or mid-term.

the immigrant group and the weak internal societal structures within the nation could quickly lead to societal friction, essentially negatively affecting overall political and societal performance and moving the nation farther away from efficient knowledge production. However, an analysis is not made to withstand time but is only a snapshot of a particular political or societal situation, meaning that the analysis of the same topic, though being a different dynamic, might produce completely different results at a different moment in time, due to the different circumstances.

In general, the purpose of political analysis is to solve political problems by finding the most suitable response in terms of enabling, restoring or improving genuine knowledge production. And again: the better the analysis, the better the policy response. However, due to the strong technocratic character of devletist systems, policymaking does not consider policy effects on certain groups of the population but rather views the nation as a whole. While much of the inefficiencies and frictions in party-based systems arise from representatives of different groups trying to defend their respective group's interests, these are eliminated in devletist systems. However, this happens, to a subjective extent, at the expense of parts of the society. Some groups will always have the feeling of being side-lined or misrepresented within technocratic governments. This happens mainly because people are much more focused on the present than the future – let alone the long-term future, which is an essential aspect of Devletism. Because devletist politics is focused on the life cycle of the nation rather than the population, it is hard for citizens to understand how particular policy courses relate to them and their desired prosperity and well-being. As mentioned earlier, if a devletist government adheres to the principles of this school, the effects of security, prosperity and well-being are being accounted for, simply because they can be considered as enabling factors for devletist governance. It might not be perceived that way periodically and sometimes there is regression but the success of a nation cannot be compromised by short-term considerations of convenience.

Chapter XIII

Culture as the Third Pillar of Political Analysis

Next to the long-term approach and the centrality of technical, political analysis within devletist systems, another pillar of devletist policymaking is the alignment of policy outputs with the cultural core of the respective society. Earlier, the concept of culture was explored, identifying it as the building block of societies, states, governments and nations. Viewing culture in the context of policymaking brings us back to the philosophical underpinnings of Devletism, which are grounded in the assumption that every person has a special trait which she is ought to find and develop, as well as to produce genuine knowledge through the translation of this trait into real-world outputs. Similarly, because societies are composed of people, it is only natural that they, too, have such a special trait, or set of distinct characteristics, which are derived from the aggregate tendencies of that society's population. We call this set of distinct characteristics of a society *culture*. One can easily derive from that, societies, just as individuals, need to identify their culture, become familiar with it and translate it into real-world outcomes, which is politics in this case. Just like the special trait of individuals gives them an unquantifiable advantage over others, enabling them to further society through their craft, culture is practically the unique identity of a society that enables it to advance with certain focal points, in which other societies might struggle to advance at a similar development rate. This is not to say that states should neglect other policy areas, but rather that the whole policy process needs to be adjusted to the core properties of a society's culture, in order to extract maximum value from policymaking and developing more efficiently and sustainably. Moreover, if policymaking is not reflective of or not in harmony with a society's culture, it will ultimately lead to the demise of the nation.

Therefore, a main precondition of genuine knowledge production by means of politics, and equally important as technocratic governance, is the consciousness about the society's culture – its society's distinct character. Culture was defined as a set of social interactions within an ethnic group. It follows that the political system needs to identify these social interactions, in order to filter out the social characteristics of its people. The component of the ethnic group requires the political system to be aware of the natural characteristics of its people. Both aspects are subject to change, which is a sign of a healthy society, given that the development is organic and not driven by external forces. Externally imposed change is one of the most common factors that leads to the decline of civilisations. However, also an internally driven decline of civilisations is possible if the political system is drifting too far away from the cultural core of its society. Here, the political system can no longer fulfil the most fundamental task of governance, namely ensuring the nation's survival. This phenomenon is called decadence and is another very common cause of societal collapse.[32] Summarising, we can say that the decline of societies can be divided into a decline caused by external factors, such as war, and internal factors, namely decadence.

If we are to draw a parallel at the individual level to better understand the connection between a society's success and politics in alignment with its culture, we can think about a person who has not found her special trait or found it without developing it or translating it into outcomes. This person will never be able to experience the feeling of true fulfilment. Of course, she might be happy, satisfied and even successful but because she did not reach fulfilment, she has not achieved the purpose of her life, making her death an ultimate one. Individuals, in turn, who were able to find, develop and realise their unique potential went on to build legacies, lasting years, decades, centuries and even millennia after their deaths. Societies that lose their connection to their cultural core – may it be through internal or external factors – are bound to vanish sooner or later.

---

[32] The most prominent example is the fall of the Roman Empire. Due to its long-lasting decline and ultimate collapse, the Ottoman Empire could also be described as a decadent system.

The best example of a successful society which has been able to survive over three millennia, is the Jewish society. Interestingly, over much of their existence, Jews did not have a core territory that they consistently ruled over nor did they own an outright state for a long period – let alone built a lasting Jewish nation under a stable state structure.[33] Nonetheless, they were not only able to survive but also managed to become an incredibly powerful and successful society as well as one of the societies which greatly contributed to genuine knowledge production. The reason for the great success of the Jewish people is that they have a clearly identified understanding of who is considered a Jew.[34] Further, they have a strong common sense around what constitutes Jewish culture which helped them to achieve and maintain a high internal social cohesiveness. A central aspect is that Jews were able to structure their behaviour around this awareness of their culture, making them operate at an efficiency rate close to their true potential. One major advantage, which aided the aforementioned factors, is the existence of a common manifesto – the Torah. It not only explains the origins of the Jewish people but also formulates a normative set of social

---

[33] It was only after 1948 that the Jewish society could establish a state that fulfilled the criteria outlined in Article 1 of the Montevideo Conference (1933).

[34] Within Jewish culture, it is well established and legally manifested that Jewishness is transferred through matrilineality (see Mishnah, Kiddushin 3:12).

interactions within this ethnic group.[35] As we know from the previous parts, a set of social interactions within an ethnic group is called culture. Therefore, the Torah is the manifestation of Jewish culture – a cultural constitution so to say. While it should be acknowledged that the Torah also holds spiritual value, it is more of a cultural work than a religious one. Other religions try to set out universal rules and guidelines, which is why anyone can adopt them. Religions, however, are organically born out of specific cultural circumstances and they all must be understood as cultural manifestos by means of a spiritual message, even though the intention of most religions was to formulate universal rules. Although the aim is the universal application of the formulated rules, in reality, those rules are most effective within that very cultural context they originated in. To my knowledge, no religion is centred around one ethnic group – except for Judaism. The misuse of religions and societal disruptions that follow the imposition, or the voluntary adoption, of religions with non-organic origins on other cultures are caused by a misalignment between the cultural core of the society adopting the religion and the normative principles of such a religion. In the

---

[35] In comparison to many other works after the Torah, the Torah is relatively indirect. The formulations of laws and rules based on the Torah, such as the Mishnah, Halakha, Shulchan Aruch or the Talmud, are very specific and, therefore, applicable in daily life. Nonetheless, they are complementary texts to the Torah, without which the existence of following works would not have been possible. Accordingly, the Torah is used as the central point of reference here.

long run, adopting a religion with external origins will inevitably lead to the collapse of the society.

Now, in terms of finding and incorporating the core cultural characteristics into the political system, there is a structural conflict that needs to be resolved. On the one side, the organic dynamics of cultural change need to stem from the societal interaction of its people. If the political system was to manage the course of societal change, which is also a common characteristic of contemporary democracies, the society moves farther away from its core and, thus, closer to its demise. However, politics cannot be purely reactionary but needs to proactively seek innovation, too. Also, the interactions between government and society are interconnected. Policies are inherently influencing cultural characteristics – it is literally the main task of politics to alter the behaviour of the society. With the complexity of our species, we cannot yet account for much of the effects altered behaviour would have on the cultural structure.

Now, if we are to adopt a thinking that the culture must be preserved at any cost, this paves the way for radicalism and stagnation. Politicians will try to prevent any little deviation from what they perceive to be the cultural core or what is potentially enshrined constitutionally. Allowing change is then simply a matter of interpretation on the side of the government. This is a major flaw and significantly endangers the fragile balance of any political system. If a state is vested with powers to define the cultural boundaries or even the cultural identity of a society, its organic development cannot follow its natural path and is dependent on the talent and goodwill of the specific cadre of politicians who is defining the identity. Going even further, the government would be able to move the society away from realising its potential – intentionally or unintentionally. The state should embody the ideals of the nation and its society, in order to ensure their survival and development; the government is merely the executing arm of these aims. Sooner or later, even the most skilled politicians will be replaced by a cadre of less capable people. If vested with powers that allow them to alter the course of cultural development, they will significantly harm the nation.

Chapter XIV

About the Cultural Constitution and its Importance

Nonetheless, there needs to be a constant that functions as the bridge between society and state. Its purpose is to ensure policymaking remains in line with the cultural core of the society. The easiest way is the isolation of an ethnic group. By ensuring a high internal homogeneity within a nation, the political system structurally limits the risk of external dynamics which could hamper the organic evolution of the society. Successful contemporary examples are the Scandinavian countries. Because of their geographical isolation and the harsh natural conditions of their lands, which make those countries less attractive for immigration, the Scandinavian countries were able to preserve a high degree of ethnic homogeneity.[36] In such a case, there is little outside influence that could affect social dynamics. The culture is naturally preserved. All changes and developments are mostly organic because there is little inorganic to influence them. So, when new societal trends evolve within those nations, we can be relatively sure that there is an internal change process within the

---

[36] Available data shows that in Norway, for example, the percentage of foreigners was approximately around 1,74 % in 1910. Accounts from the other Scandinavian countries do not reach that far back but numbers from Sweden show that in 1960 2,50 % of the population were foreign citizens. Denmark´s statistical reach dates back to the first quarter of 2008 where around 6,22 % of the population.

normative framework of that culture. Only a culture that changes organically remains a healthy culture. This also implies the necessity of change. No change is just as detrimental to a society as inorganic changes.

Now, not all nations have the geographical advantage of the Scandinavian nations. Further, those nations recently had to face increased immigration which started to raise concerns within the societies, due to the new situation of increased contact with external cultures. An example of isolation of a geographically non-isolated nation is China. The Chinese state is keen on preserving internal ethnic homogeneity by limiting immigration and strengthening internal cohesiveness. However, China uses brutal methods to maintain this course of social policy. Strict re-education policies, imposed political ideology and relocation policies are to be counted as rather lax policy courses, compared to ethnic elimination and genocides which are equally utilised by the Chinese state to uphold the ethnic homogeneity within its borders. Accordingly, China is rather a tyranny than a sustainable political system. Of course, much of China's economic and power political success stems from this internal cohesiveness, but it happens at the expense of quality of life. Also, it moves the nation farther away from genuine knowledge production because by wiping out other ethnicities and strictly guiding the cultural life of the own ethnicity, those people cannot fulfil their natural purpose in life. In China and similar political systems, only if the special trait of an individual happens to be aligned with government policies, a person might reach fulfilment. By doing so, China forgoes the massive potential that other ethnicities within Chinese borders could develop and ultimately add to societal progression of the Chinese nation.

The example of China shows how dangerous the isolationist approach to incorporating culture into policymaking is. Even the most sophisticated system could eventually develop brutal tendencies, in an attempt to preserve ethnic homogeneity and social cohesiveness. Policymaking should not be aimed at other societies but needs to find solutions by proactively engaging with the own society.

Following the Jewish example, every society should have a manifested set of cultural core properties: a cultural constitution. It is a proactive way to achieve culture-encompassing policymaking without discriminating against other cultures. It also enables the free cultural exchange between societies, while anchoring the own cultural properties. However, creating such a cultural constitution is of unmatched difficulty, due to a number of reasons. First, because of its massive importance to the course of societal development, it not only needs to perfectly encompass the ethnic group's culture at the time of writing but also needs to put it into writing unambiguously. How can we, at any point in time, ensure that such a constitution is not misunderstood or even misused in centuries to come? How can we account for any contingencies? Most importantly, who can truly claim to have formulated a cultural constitution that fully manifests the culture of an ethnic group, creates a meaningful set of behavioural guidelines and sets out a common vision around which societal conduct is centred?[37] Can it be that the Jewish example was just a matter of luck which cannot be repeated?

These are sensitive questions, yet of unmatched importance, due to the centrality of culturally aligned policymaking. We always need to remember that the most effective and efficient political system is one that is not only designed in harmony with the cultural core of a society but also needs to continuously perform in harmony with that core. Again, due to the philosophical understanding of the special traits of individuals, which translate into a culture on the aggregate level, the fulfilment of a nation's purpose is inherently linked to finding, developing and translating these cultural core propositions into real outcomes.

Regarding the questions about who should write such a manifesto and in what way, these depend on the respective cultural context. While in nations, like China, the laws are the written guidelines provided by the government, the Jewish cultural manifesto was written by, so they claim, a single person

---

[37] Undeniably, these are the same questions that most religions are confronted with.

some millennia ago.[38] In other contexts, like Iran or Saudi-Arabia, policymaking is tied to another cultural manifesto: the Qur'an. Here, the governments formulate laws according to the rules and guidelines from the book, which was also written by a single person, according to the Muslim teachings.

However, what can be more universally dealt with is what a cultural manifesto consists of, how it functions and how it can be integrated into policymaking. Generally, a cultural manifesto is a collection and summary of the key historic developments of that very ethnic group. It should describe the historic origins of the ethnicity, the geography it originated in and important milestones in the development of that ethnicity into a society and maybe even a nation. Every nation will have experienced times of struggle in its history. The cultural manifesto needs to emphasise these moments of the society's history, in order to create a feeling of belonging that emerges when people overcome difficult situations together. This forms a bond between the people. But also, achievements, myths and legends throughout the history of that ethnicity need to be picked up and described. Whether it is the formation of different states, wars fought, famines survived, diasporas experienced or dictatorships that the nation has

---

[38] Though the teachings are extensively examined, commented and translated into laws by many people, the main work, the Torah, is claimed to be written by a person named Moses. Not only the Jewish community believes this unanimously but also the Muslim and Christian communities share this view.

suffered under, all are part of the history of a people. Every history is unique and cannot be claimed by any other ethnic group than the respective ethnic group itself. Because of that, it is an essential part of the ethnic identity and culture. Just as our personal life experiences form our character and our relationship with our individual special trait, the ethnic history is the unique factor, that shapes how we interact with each other as the experiences of the past form our traditions, customs, way of talking and thinking and many other aspects of culture. From this, we can also observe certain societal tendencies and from them we can derive the special traits or characteristics of that society.

We could look at the Arabs, for example. Their ethnic history played exclusively in the deserts of South-West Asia and North Africa. Deserts are characterised by a calming atmosphere and clear skies. Especially at night, the sky is a fascinating phenomenon. It is not surprising that an ethnic group which lives under these conditions develops a special relationship with the night sky, which is even symbolically reflected in most Muslim nations' flags through the crescent moon. Based on that special relationship, most of the scientific advances in the fields of astronomy originated in the Arab world. In order to quantify the findings, they developed the numerical system, which is widely used today. Of course, this is just a very small and simplistic example of one aspect of an ethnic group's history, but it could be a central aspect of a cultural manifesto if they would not already have the Qur'an. The Greeks would presumably have a lot to collect on their ancestors who advanced political theory and philosophy (including the Greek Mythology) but also about the times when they were ruled by the Ottoman Empire, which is also an essential factor that influenced the society and its culture.

Every nation is born out of a society and every society has lived through a history that made an ethnic group become this very society. How one led to the other is an essential and unique property of every nation and, hence, a defining one in terms of culture. Collecting and manifesting this knowledge gives the people a point of reference and policymaking a broad frame to shape policy outcomes in a way that is harmonic and consistent with that past. Certainly, there is a lot of room for interpretation whether policymaking is a logical continuation of history and there is surely more than one suitable path that fulfils this requirement, but a relatively clearly defined national identity should suffice to recognise when policymaking is moving towards a disconnection from that past. It does not follow that traditions, customs and views should be preserved at all costs. Rather, the opposite is the case. There must be change and development, for the nation to continuously engage in genuine knowledge production, but it must happen within the harmonic frame of the nation's culture, in order to move closer to the full utilisation of its potential.

This leads us to the second aspect of cultural manifestos. Within the history of the ethnic group, there must be a common goal, a vision or a prophecy. Usually, such documents will claim a certain importance or superiority of the addressed people over other ethnicities or religions. In the Torah, for example, it is claimed that the Jews are the chosen people by a higher spiritual instance and that a certain territory is inherently ascribed to them.[39] This is something that brings a people even closer together because they are jointly striving to achieve this goal. Since they direct their lives towards the same goal, it only makes sense that they are moving in this direction together. In Islam, the goal is to reach paradise.[40] In other religions, which are, as seen above, not more than cultural manifestos within a specific cultural context, self-awareness or other personal experiences are central. Such a common vision could even be that a society strives to become the nation of music or art because that is what defines their existence. The key aspect for policymaking is that the policy output must embrace this common goal, vision or prophecy. Just as the history, common goal, vision or prophecy of a society is unique and, therefore, defining of the identity and culture of that society, policies must be logical steps towards the achievement of these normative ideals. By doing so,

---

[39] Deuteronomy 4:20.

[40] The word paradise is mentioned 147 times in the Qur´an and the ultimate reward for a righteously lived life on earth, according to the teachings.

policymaking is operating at a high rate of efficiency because it remains aligned with the cultural core of the society.

A third aspect of cultural manifestos is a formulated set of values. Every religious, ethnic, political or cultural work will seek to outline a normative framework. Here, questions about right and wrong, good and bad, honourable and dishonourable are answered. Most apparent is this part of cultural manifestos in religious works which often clearly formulate rules of behaviour that followers of that religion need to adhere to. Sometimes the philosophical background of those behavioural rules is explained but more often there are just dogmatic rules. Nonetheless, they provide a useful point of reference to better define the culture of a society and serve as the normative basis of that society's judicial system.[41] While the common history and goal of an ethnic group are unique aspects, the normative framework is not solely confined to one society. Many societies condemn, for example, polygamy or murder. To name a positive example, many cultures also embrace their elders and pay much respect to them. These aspects alone do not define the cultural core or societal identity but are complementing aspects to the common history and common goal. Staying with the example of respecting elders, the form, in which this respect is expressed, can greatly differ from

---

[41] Chapter XXV discusses this aspect in great detail as it is central to the structure of the devletist judiciary.

society to society. It underlines that the behavioural rules are aspects that stem from the unique history and the common goal. Because it might be difficult for people to derive useful behavioural guidance from historic events by themselves, the normative framework is a hands-on mechanism that translates the unique aspects of the cultural manifesto into tangible concepts for all members of society. This is especially useful for policymaking as politicians would be bound to respect the boundaries of the norms, values and principles outlined in the manifesto. Because it is easier to determine whether a policy is infringing cultural norms, values or principles than to assess whether a policy is a logical step in the pursuit to achieve the common goal, this normative framework provides a more reliable point of reference to assess policy performance. Moreover, by structuring the judiciary around this aspect of the cultural manifesto, there is another strong factor that adds to the translation of words into deeds.

The last aspect of cultural manifestos, and somewhat interconnected with the previous point, is the translation of norms, values and principles into traditions and customs. By preserving and developing certain traditions, a certain degree of historic continuity is achieved. Also, it strengthens the cultural identity and cohesiveness. This is because traditions and customs are a form of communication that is unique to an ethnic group. By practising them, people communicate in a way that only they can fully comprehend as they are grounded in a common understanding of the practise. For policymaking, traditions are less relevant than the first three aspects of cultural manifestos. Traditions are rather symbolic acts and do not influence policy performance, when practised by politicians publicly. As such, they are more important to interpersonal conduct, but it must be mentioned that most traditions arise from the first three pillars of cultural manifestos, which makes traditions conceptually subordinate to them.

For policymaking the history of the ethnic group, its common goal, vision or prophecy, and the normative framework are the most important aspects. A devletist government will need to respect these aspects and incorporate them into its policymaking. It is not a contradiction to technocratic governance, as some might argue, because a society can only engage in genuine knowledge production if it advances in harmony with its cultural core. The cultural manifesto is a way of structuring the political course positively and proactively around this cultural core, hindering the society from drifting away from its identity and, thus, into ineffective policymaking.

Chapter XV

Introduction to the Six Policy Areas

The structures and principles that we have explored together, up to this point, serve as a solid basis for a successful political system. Broadly speaking, the voting system ensures the proper staffing of government posts, while the principles of policymaking set the broad frame within which it should move. Most importantly, the view that states should build their policymaking around the assumption that our purpose of existence is to enhance through genuine knowledge production rectifies an age-old misunderstanding about the tasks of the state and, hence, provides us with a clearly defined goal. However, we can move yet closer to progressive policymaking by exploring the respective policy areas on the structural level as well as on the content level. The attentive reader might be puzzled by this statement as just in the previous parts the importance of culture-oriented policymaking was stressed. We could interpret the analysis of policymaking on the content level as a contradiction to culture-based policymaking since formulating rules to the specific content might produce a conflict with what is best from the cultural perspective. An example, which summarises this dilemma quite neatly, can be found in economics. It could be stated that a healthy economy must focus on heavy industry.

However, all those nations with less abundant raw materials would have a hard time to expand their heavy industry, and even if they still tried to engage in such expansionary efforts, it would be much more costly for them, due to the increased procurement cost of those missing raw materials. This cost inefficiency will significantly reduce a nation's competitiveness and its chances of building an effective system. Culture-based policymaking would suggest identifying economic strengths and developing those to a point where the development of weaker sectors, such as heavy industry in this example, becomes more cost-efficient.

How can we then make assessments on the content-level if much of effective policymaking is based on the specific circumstances of the respective societies? Reusing the example of the economic structure of a nation, we could say that any economy needs to have a well-regulated financial system. The reason for the validity of this claim, in comparison to the previous claim on heavy industries, is that a financial system with little systemic downside risk will always be able to attract new capital to the economy – especially in times of crisis. Further, it will reduce the probability of systemic economic failures, while at the same time serving as a basis for sustainable economic growth. Without compromising the aspect of culture-based policymaking, this claim can be sustained in any context and serves as a solid guideline for any nation. It is, admittedly, a fine line that needs to be preserved, as not all aspects of policymaking can be assessed as unambiguously as in the previous example. Another aspect to consider is that rulers might misuse the notion of culture-based politics by framing their personally desired course of policy action as if it is in line with the society's culture, even though this might not be true and, in the worst case, even harmful to the nation. Because this aspect is a rather qualitative and even emotional part of policymaking, manipulation of public opinion can be more easily channelled through acts under the pretext of culture-based politics. Therefore, examining more general principles within the policy areas becomes all the more important, even if the difficulty of avoiding contradiction with some cultural properties persists. However, the following parts aim to find a suitable balance between preserving room for culture-based policymaking on the one hand and technocratic policymaking on the other.

In the following chapters, six policy areas will be explored on this basis. Another methodological choice, that was made here, are the respective policy areas and their division into six distinct areas, which are: *education, economy and finance, foreign policy, environment and urban planning, welfare system* and, ultimately, *the judiciary*. It does not automatically follow that government ministries need to be reduced to the number of six, as there can be certainly more ministries that administer sub-areas of the respective policy fields. For example, there can potentially be a ministry entrusted with the nation's policies on transportation and infrastructure, while this ministry's competences would fall under the umbrella of the policy area of environment and urban planning for some, others would link it to the field of economy and finance. To varying degrees, the policy areas and the ministries are interdependent and interconnected, but structuring the ministries along the lines of the respective policy areas will help professionals, citizens and scholars to better grasp the purpose and functioning of the policies within that policy field. Such a categorisation also facilitates the understanding of state competences.

The rest of this work is devoted to the six policy areas in the order in which they are enlisted above, beginning with education. Before we begin, it should be mentioned that education is the most important policy area of them all, which is why it will receive special attention. This makes especially sense since the purpose of the state – and, even more so, our entire existence – is based on the production of genuine knowledge. Education is the cornerstone of policymaking and the basis of survival of any nation. It can be safely said that all other policy areas – and this will become even clearer in the latter course of this work – are designed in a way that enables the area of education to function at the highest level of effectiveness and efficiency.

Chapter XVI

About the Centrality of Education within Devletism

Education is the most important aspect of devletist governance. It is defined as the process of finding and developing the special trait that lies at the centre of every individual's personality. Certainly, this definition is very different from other schools of thought, which do not include the notion of the special trait in their teachings, or at least do not centre their theories around this notion. However, a general definition will not suffice for our purposes here. Neither would it make much sense to compromise the utility of the term, in order to press it into a predefined frame which would lead to more confusion within the understanding of this work. By tying education to the notion of the special trait, it is directly linked to the purpose of our existence. Without education, we will not be able to find our special trait and without developing this trait, we will not be able to reach mastery in the exercise of it, which is essential. Imagining the pity one would feel for a great scientist, writer, politician or artist who never produced outcomes beyond the quality of her first work neatly illustrates the importance of perfecting the craft, whatever it might be. Education is the basis on which this development happens.

In the context of policymaking, education needs to be translated into a systematic institutional framework which facilitates the process of finding and developing this special trait of individuals. This is, in theory, equally possible without an institutional framework. However, the efficiency is greatly increased because such a framework provides pooled assets to this important process and, thus, enables the members of the society access to expertise, learning materials, structured learning, exchange with peers, enhanced methodologies and training in scientific conduct. In simplified terms, an education system can be viewed as a training camp for the acquisition of existing knowledge, which would probably take some additional decades to accumulate, before one would be able to start producing new knowledge if done individually. On the practical side, it creates a system of reference, which is important for other society members to broadly categorise another person's capabilities. This is especially useful in economic terms because it reduces the transaction costs of trial and error which would arise when economic actors were to employ people without a frame of reference to assess the skills and capabilities of people, provided by the education system through a grading system. Further, it also facilitates international scientific and economic conduct, since the quantification of educational progress functions as an important point of reference.

Returning to the domestic structures of the education system, a state's role is to provide the necessary funding, institutions and processes for the society members to find their special traits and develop them. A successful education system, therefore, is one in which as many people as possible find their special trait and are able to become masters in what they do. The better the education system operates the more people will work closely to their full potential. It follows that when as many people as possible are operating close to their full potential, the society functions close to its objective potential. Maybe the greatest advantage of this approach is its self-reconstructive characteristic. When the development of each individual is the focus of policymaking, the invested resources in this development are simultaneously investments in the resolution of all other policy problems at once, providing the best return on investment. By broadly increasing the quality of individual output, the resolution of current and future problems will be more effective, and the crafting of new policies will produce less flawed outcomes in the first place.

Chapter XVII

The Education System under Devletism

Although humans greatly differ, there are some core aspects of our being that are constant throughout all ethnicities. One is that we are going through different cognitive development stages and socialisation processes. Accordingly, effective development must be in harmony with the respective stages of growing up. The needs and capabilities of children change over time and a good education system addresses those needs and poses challenges for the children to test their capabilities. In the early stages of life (at least until the age of seven), the single most important aspect is to shield children from negative influences. This does not mean that children should not experience any inconveniences, such as not getting an item they desperately want or minor confrontations with peers, which are important for our social functioning, but rather that they should not be exposed to structurally negative events or behaviour. In other words, we could also describe it as shielding children from negative and destructive energies. Violence, divorce of the parents, careless parents, lack of basic material needs, aggressive people in the close environment and other negative situations and events can have lasting effects on children, although it is unclear in what particular ways they will impair future development. Surely, the state has limited tools to provide a secure environment for children at home, and here it is a matter of culture-oriented policymaking to decide to what degree a state should have the possibility to intervene in intra-family affairs, but one universal necessity is that children need to always be surrounded by a positive, supportive and secure environment throughout all stages of their institutional education but especially in their *early education* until the age of seven.

Education at this stage should be characterised by play and fostering social interaction. Learning, here, is centred around exploring the world, understanding basic concepts within it and internalising fundamental socio-cultural interactions. It is very important that children learn to build and maintain connections to their peers and surroundings because this forms our interpersonal behaviour that we have to live with for the rest of our lives. The teachers' responsibility is to ensure inclusion of all children in the respective groups. As mentioned earlier, the connection to their surroundings is equally important. By enabling children to establish contact with nature and animals, their degree of empathy is greatly improved. In general, it is important that the education system provides opportunities for children to discover many different positive aspects of life. In terms of genuine knowledge production, this is the stage where first tendencies of children's special traits become visible. Because our special trait is something we inherently carry within ourselves since birth, it should not come by surprise that first tendencies can be identified quite early. However, this can only happen to many children if the institutional education enables them to have contact with many different areas of life, such as nature, arts, literature, animals, music, technical and mechanical things, biology and many other areas.

In addition to that, the teachers must also be able to recognise certain tendencies in child behaviour. Only then will they be able to support every child's development in that respective area. So, it is not merely sufficient for teachers to provide opportunities for exploring the world, but they will have to identify the children's special interests and give them the chance to have more contact with those areas that they are talented in. A child that seems to show a special interest in buildings should have increased contact with games and activities that are connected to buildings, construction and architecture. What becomes clear here is that teachers have a crucial role in the whole development process of children. It is, therefore, necessary to properly train teachers. The requirements for becoming a teacher must be very high, both technically and socially. Along with having a proper academic background, they must possess a high degree of intrinsic motivation and empathy, which needs to be constantly monitored as well as maintained through proper incentives. Accordingly, the pay levels must reflect the level of expectation, to create a material incentive for future teachers; the normative satisfaction of training future generations will not be sufficient to attract motivated teachers and keep them motivated throughout their careers. This also holds true for teachers and professors in the following stages of institutional education. Because the role of teachers is so crucial for societal progress, this profession needs to be especially honoured, but also strictly monitored.

Concluding the design of the institutional education in the early stage of child development, the school facilities need to be addressed, too. Again, this is an aspect where universal principles can be applied. As mentioned earlier, at this stage of child development, the importance of positivity is stressed. The school buildings must reflect that and create a positive and cosy atmosphere. From an architectural perspective, the facilities must allow a lot of light to enter the school buildings. Decorations should be colourful, artistic and creative. Here, the children can be included to produce artwork which adorn the walls and floors. This helps to foster the fantasy of the children and is a wonderful way for them to channel their creative drive into real outcomes early on. Tables, chairs, boards, toys and other objects should be made of high-quality materials spreading a calm and warm energy. All these aspects subconsciously influence children and should be used to complement the playful and positive atmosphere of early-stage development.

This also applies to the second stage of education at which children experience their first contact with structured learning. This second stage – *the primary education stage* –, comprises the institutionalisation of education for children between the ages seven to twelve. However, this should not be taken as a universal rule. Primary education could also range from seven to ten, for example. The lowest level for dividing early-stage education and primary education should be the age of seven, while it should range until the age of twelve, at the latest. Between these ages, the basic socialisation process is completed and children become more receptive to fundamental technical concepts, such as reading, writing and simple maths. Of course, entering this second stage, socialisation and play will remain core focal points but should gradually make place for more material learning. Again, a broad range of topics should be touched upon by the teachers, which is why the division into certain subjects takes place at this level. Language, maths, natural sciences, physical education, arts and music are the core aspects that the children need to build a basic understanding of. These topics should, again, be approached in a playful and creative way. Neither homework should not be part of learning at this stage nor the quantitative assessment of skills. It is particularly important that education does not receive a compulsive character, but rather consolidates itself as something intrinsically desirable in the minds of children. Certainly, not every child will approach every subject with the same enthusiasm but by freely roaming through the world of knowledge, children should develop a minimum level of interest in many subjects. By doing so, children will also naturally move closer to the subjects of their inherent interest that stems from their special trait, while building an awareness of the interconnected nature of our being. Teachers are responsible for enabling children to dive further into subjects of their individual interest.

Another important building block for the effective achievement of the abovementioned aspects is the utilisation of practical tasks. By involving children in the process of solution-finding, they will be able to develop a comprehensive understanding of the things they are dealing with. Experiments and projects are great ways to include children in the process. It will be surprising to see for teachers and parents how creative the approaches of children can be, and this should be preserved and encouraged at all costs. Moreover, there will be enough time in the later stages of their lives to follow stricter patterns of knowledge accumulation, training and scientific conduct.

Another important aspect to consider at this, and the following educational stages, is that children will be able to read, and knowledge will also be increasingly transmitted through textbooks and other learning materials. Therefore, it is important that the design and the content of those materials remain positive and does not contain subliminal messages. Unfortunately, almost all education systems use connotative tools to subconsciously shape the perception of children. Through word choice, selection of example questions and depiction of characters, the education system transmits subliminal messages on the basis of a political agenda. Education must be freed from this. It is a cowardly way to attack the norms and values that lay at the core of every society because children are significantly more prone to be influenced by those tactics and are defenceless against this kind of manipulation. Education must never be a political tool. Under Devletism, education is an end in itself.

This aspect serves as a transition to the next level of education because it equally applies to all the following stages of institutional education. After completing the primary education stage, children are equipped with basic knowledge on a broad range of subjects. In terms of socialisation, children should now have developed a more distinct character and should master the advanced forms of communication and cooperation. *The secondary education stage* now serves as the level where knowledge is further solidified, extended and should gradually become more complex towards the end of this stage. From an institutional perspective, secondary education should begin around the ages of eleven or twelve and extend to the ages of eighteen to twenty years. Here too, the specific institutional design can vary. The core purpose at this level is to prepare students to master more complex cognitive tasks. Attending this educational stage must be mandatory. However, the system should not be designed in a way that enables all students to complete this stage – let alone graduate with a good grade. The reason for it is that the content should be highly challenging. It is better for students to receive low grades for great cognitive achievements than receiving good grades for mediocre achievements. As it is with things in life, a healthy degree of pressure is necessary to constantly be challenged to become a better person. In the end, the quality of education determines the quality of societal progress, and a challenging educational path is necessary to stress the seriousness of education. In the light of the previous educational stages, students will have a certain degree of intrinsic motivation, anyway. Hence, challenging cognitive boundaries will be welcomed by the students.

The playful character will move further in the background as material aspects of education become more important. One being the mode of assessment, which will be introduced at the secondary level. Having a frame of reference for the assessment of cognitive abilities in the respective subjects is not only useful and necessary for future employers and universities to have an idea about students' capabilities but also important for the students to give them a context for their personal self-reflexion. It puts their knowledge in context of what is expected, which, in turn, is based on existing knowledge. By the age of fifteen, for instance, a student might feel that she has grasped certain concepts to the fullest, but this is never the case. Quantifying it at the secondary education level will help her understand that there is much more to the specific subjects than she can currently grasp.

Additionally, like this, teachers can better identify tendencies and potentially the special traits of students. This will help them to support the development in these areas. Again, in terms of specific grading designs and fostering development in the areas of the individual special traits, the education must find a way to structure it in a way that encompasses the cultural core. Societies inherently differ in their intra-cultural conduct, which needs to be reflected here. Some systems might prefer grading on practical assignments, while others rather rely on oral or written examinations. Some might favour punctual examination systems, while others grade longer performance periods. There is no universal key to grading.

One of the things that serves as a guiding principle is that the education plan needs to be ambitious without relying on by heart learning or becoming too descriptive. Another important aspect is that grading needs to be fair and unbiased. Intuitively, we tend to think about ethnic discrimination at schools where foreigners are downgraded, due to the underlying tendencies to strengthen social cohesion on the side of the majority. However, also other forms of bias are very common in school systems. Especially, the bias towards financially well-backed students is a great problem. Certainly, a lot has to do with the fact that economic power most often increases the social status of people in contemporary and past societies. Within devletist systems, where elitist structures are more likely to evolve around academic achievements (let us think about the voting system which is built on knowledge), the economic bias towards students is greatly reduced. However, it might well come to a situation where teachers start to treat children from families with greater academic success more favourably, which is also undesirable. Three mechanisms could reduce, though unlikely eliminate, this potential bias as well as the previously described existing biases. First, anonymous examination processes can help, where suitable, preventing teachers from favouring or discriminating certain students. However, if the mode of assessment is based on oral examination or tracks long-term performance, this is significantly more difficult and sometimes even impossible. Second, teachers' pay needs to be very high, as mentioned earlier. With increased pay, the performance pressure on teachers increases. Further, because teachers are paid with tax money, the increased salary also increases the accountability of teachers. Parents will be much more sensitive towards teacher-student dynamics and are more likely to hold teachers accountable, due to the increased stake in teachers' pay. Third, teacher performance needs to be closely monitored by the ministry of education. Not only is this necessary because the content and mode of transmitting knowledge needs to adhere to the highest standards, but also to ensure that teachers enable all students the possibility of unfolding their potential. The ways of monitoring teachers can be very different. One good way is to frequently visit classes randomly and observe the teachers' behaviour. Here, the respective authorities practically surprise the teacher, who will not have the chance to prepare herself for the visit. The more such a visit happens on a random basis the more likely teachers are to adapt their behaviour to the expected standard. However, passive monitoring is equally important. Schools should always allow their students to voice their concerns, bring up points of critique or point to problems in classes. Such complaints need to be taken seriously and at least lead to a closer examination of the situation.

By the end of the secondary education stage, students will have completed the fundamental education process. From here, it is up to them to decide whether they want to directly enter the labour market or continue their academic endeavour by attending university. Both paths are equally acceptable in personal terms as long as those young people stay dedicated to whatever craft they are performing. However, it must be stated that *university education* receives a positive bias under Devletism. This is because at the university level the level of complexity of cognitive tasks is considerably higher than anywhere else. As nations aim at advancing genuine knowledge production, universities are at the forefront of this process, due to their dealings with complex subject matter. One might argue that if one's special trait is in the field of arts, for instance, university education might not be necessary because it is a practical field. However, university education will help in every field of interest to deepen the knowledge on the respective subject. In the example of arts, the history and technical aspects of painting, drawing, sculpturing and other branches will be explored in great detail – things that complement the process of becoming a master in this field. The same can be applied to virtually all other professions. A carpenter, for instance, could study her craft at university level, too.

The usefulness of university or tertiary education is more visible in other areas, such as the natural or political sciences. Here, the incredibly complex works of past great minds are examined in detail and based on those findings new knowledge is created. The university is the educational institution where these efforts are channelled and transmitted by means of cooperation more efficiently. Let us just think about laboratories that are needed for researching new technologies in natural sciences. But also in the social sciences, the university provides structures, processes and materials that help us collect and process data. These are all essential parts of advancing our current pool of knowledge. There is no such thing as unnecessary knowledge. Knowledge must never be viewed from a utility perspective. Since it is an end in itself, learning and furthering knowledge in every aspect of life are inherently desirable. Universities' purpose is to do just that.

Structurally, the current and common form of university education is suitable. A Bachelor's degree over a time span of three to five years, with an optional master's degree of one to three years, in principle, suffices to develop into an expert within the field of the individual special trait; especially, when we think about the ambitious educational past students will have completed by the time of enrolment to a university. Also, the continuation of the process by pursuing a doctorate and potentially a professorship is a very suitable design for reaching mastery in any field of interest.[42]

Another structural aspect is that universities should be free of charge. Because it is so central to the purpose of the nation, it is the nation's responsibility to enable all qualifying students to enter a university. Financial concerns should not compromise students' will to pursue their dreams in the field of their special trait. Also, from a normative perspective, the philosophical underpinnings of Devletism do not allow for the state to charge its citizens to access an environment where they can fulfil their purpose of existence. It would be contradictory to say that a society's purpose is to engage in genuine knowledge production and then create financial barriers to the exercise of it at the very forefront where the significant progress is made. This leads us to another aspect: the public-private divide. Universities should not be private organisations. For one, because of the aforementioned

---

[42] It needs to be added that all university degrees must be highly challenging, on the content-level.

principle that universities should be free of charge, which private universities are not. Even if they are, they need to seek financing from other sources. Naturally, these sources of funding will then receive a stake in the university and impose its views, aspirations and interests on the institution.[43] But also without a stakeholder, every private organisation will develop an organisational interest as we have seen earlier. Just like political parties, private universities will develop intra-organisational interests which are highly unlikely to fully align with the national interests. Therefore, universities, just as all the other institutional forms of education, need to be intertwined with the state. With this system, another problem is solved, as well. In the contemporary labour market, graduates from private universities, especially expensive ones, tend to be favoured – often just for the sake of the artificial prestige of the institution. All the knowledge that is transmitted to the students at those institutions is available elsewhere, too. With the proper funding by the state, all other universities can also provide the very same learning materials. Except for the prestige, state universities provide the very same quality of education – at least they can easily do so. The prestige, on the other hand, is an artificial construct and a product of flawed political systems. At various points in this work, and most

---

[43] Certainly, such an influence is not always exerted blatantly. Sometimes it is not intended at all. However, in all cases there will be a leniency towards a favourable policy course of the donor.

recently in this chapter about teacher bias, current and past elitism based on financial considerations is also the driving factor here. Abolishing private educational institutions, just like political parties, will significantly add to levelling the playing field for academics and bring performance considerations to the foreground.

Performance is really the key component at university level education. Here, the last bit of playful education methodology is eliminated and the modes of knowledge accumulation, processing and developing into new knowledge are our sole focal points. Since the previous educational stages are aimed at enabling students to find their special trait, it can be reasonably expected that students will pursue academic studies in this very field of their inherent interest which simultaneously means that students will approach their studies with an intrinsic motivation. Such a motivation is necessary to conduct more effective academic works and to gain an unquantifiable amplifying effect of genuine knowledge production.

Just like the previous educational stages, university level education needs to be extremely challenging. However, this should not be understood as a call for a quantitative overload in terms of learning information by heart. Rather, the aim should be to challenge knowledge boundaries. A question unasked is just as bad as an answer unquestioned. Of course, much of the knowledge we possess today, and that we are holding on to, will likely be deemed invalid one day. A lot of what we know today will turn out to be untrue or incomplete. A lot of egos will be hurt, and a lot of individual interests will be infringed on such an approach. Even this work's teachings will gradually be complemented – maybe even rejected and replaced one day. However, this is a key aspect of progress. Just like this work challenges the past findings in this field, Devletism will be challenged and more effective and efficient teachings on state theory might emerge, and they, in turn, might also be challenged and replaced. Without the previous works, however, progress would not have been possible – they serve as steps on a ladder towards the understanding of the objective truth. A university is the production site of the knowledge ladder that brings us closer to this understanding. If universities do not challenge knowledge boundaries and push them further, they are obsolete.

Chapter XVIII

The Devletist Economy

The second policy area that needs to be examined from a devletist perspective is the economy. Since the education system is the most important policy area and put first, one might follow that the economy is the second most important policy area, but this is not the case. All the following policy areas are equally important to the proper functioning of a devletist system – only education is a special policy area, due to the nature of Devletism. A useful divide, that can be drawn to illustrate the importance of education, is that education is to be seen as an end in itself, while all other policy areas are means to the end of genuine knowledge production. Education is the direct exercise of genuine knowledge production, while all other actions are only enabling or supporting actions.

Economic conduct is one of them. Here, the economy is described as the aggregate of all monetised exchanges between citizens of a nation. These exchanges can be grounded in different motives, but within the framework of the devletist thought, an economy must be designed in a way to enable efficient societal progress by safeguarding and improving the material living standards, which help people to produce genuine knowledge more efficiently. Beginning from basic needs, such as food, water and shelter, to arranging a suitable workspace and obtaining materials for whatever craft is performed, economic conduct enables us to provide for these things in the most efficient way. Painters cannot paint without their brushes and canvases, musicians cannot play without their instruments and even politicians cannot work without at least a pencil and a piece of paper.

Producing those tools will cost vast amounts of time if one would try to completely avoid economic conduct and, hence, cooperation. Moreover, this is going to compromise the quality of the output. The reason for that is that we would expect the instrument manufacturer to be a person who has found her special trait in making instruments, which gives her an unquantifiable advantage over "regular" manufacturers and, in turn, makes her produce instruments of very high quality, while being efficient in the process. The quality of the instruments will influence the quality of the musician's output. However, she will not provide the instruments to the musician for free. For one, because she has invested her time, energy and laboriously acquired expertise into the production of her instruments. But also at the most basic level, she has obtained raw materials from a person whose special trait it is to provide the best raw materials and this person, too, has invested time, energy and her laboriously acquired expertise to provide the best raw materials.

Money helps to quantify the value of services and goods. If the buyer agrees to pay a certain amount for goods or a service, economic conduct happens. It reduces the transaction cost of finding agreeable terms of exchange between two or more unequal goods or services as it serves as a mediating carrier of value. Because money functions through the acceptance of the buyer, it serves as a quite accurate indicator of the value of goods and services in relation to one another – in theory. Later, we will explore why this assumption cannot be upheld under the contemporary economic circumstances. Nevertheless, money is a useful invention that helps us to focus on the process of genuine knowledge production more efficiently. Furthermore, it is also a necessary tool to provide for all other prerequisites of genuine knowledge production, such as survival. Without money, a state could not be formed – let alone be defended. The complexity of the purpose of our existence requires us to cooperate, and cooperation is not more than the rearrangement and management of resources which requires the utilisation of money.

To illustrate the usefulness of money, we can think about the state as it needs to provide for the safety of its society. This, in turn, requires a military force. Accordingly, the state needs to obtain weapons and train soldiers. Raw material, expertise and human capital are all resources that need to be rearranged and managed. However, all the involved parties and actors need to simultaneously rearrange and manage resources in their personal lives; mainly, because they need to safeguard their survival, improve their conditions of genuine knowledge production and, finally, also engage in it. Money is a mechanism that enables the efficient balancing of all those considerations because it is a universally agreed frame of reference for the value of goods, services and resources, serving as the basis on which rearrangement and management can happen. Without it, it would be difficult to build a military force and keep it operable. The same is also applicable to any other organisational arrangement.

Now, if we think about the economy in the light of the factors above, one might quickly come to the conclusion that the state needs to centrally administer the economy because the purpose of the economy needs to be aligned with the societal purpose. However, we have numerous historic examples of failed state management of economies, and this is not merely to be explained by the inability of the respective political cadres.[44] There is a structural argument that speaks against state-controlled economies: the special trait. People's behaviour is intrinsically driven by personal preferences, talents and tendencies. Even if we are not aware of our special trait, there are reasons for our economic behaviour, such as buying preferences, the jobs we want to work at or the degree of success we have (or do not have) economically. A state-controlled economy where nearly all

---

[44] The most prominent example being the Soviet Union.

economic conduct is planned is inherently inefficient because it will hinder many citizens to behave naturally; simply, because it is impossible to centrally place every citizen at her most efficient economic place. Any unnatural behaviour is unsustainable – a notion that is central to devletist thinking. Therefore, the economy needs to allow people to behave naturally, within certain borders, however. Money enables such natural behaviour and is, therefore, a key component within a decentralised economy because it allows actors to freely agree on prices which creates dynamic buying and selling incentives. It is a practical tool because it reduces the transaction cost of negotiation.

Another important cornerstone of the economy is private property. Since it is impossible for a state to employ every citizen at her most efficient place within the economy, we can reasonably argue that it is also impossible for a state to efficiently decide the efficient distribution of all resources, either. Private property enables individuals to obtain, manage and redistribute resources to their best knowledge which should be in accordance with their individual nature. Therefore, a free economy is an efficient mechanism. Through action and reaction, the system will stay in a natural equilibrium. All these principles are fundamental in conservative economics, however, the devletist view is different as there are some key structural changes that alter this economic view. Here, it cannot be stressed enough that one should not equate the devletist economy with the purely free market economy and even less so should the devletist economy be described as a free market economy without centring the debate around concepts that will follow shortly.

Before, it was stressed that a functioning economy is based on citizen's ability to act in accordance with their individual nature. This makes sense especially in the light of the assumption that every person has a special trait inherent to her. However, in contemporary economies, which are mostly free market economies, we can observe that they strongly favour economic actors with more economic means. Today, the more economic means are available, the more means of genuine knowledge production are available, either; a situation contrary to the thinking that the society should advance as a whole. Since genuine knowledge production is tied to the exercise of our individual special trait, it means that, within this contemporary order, more economic means lead to more and better chances to exercise and develop one's special trait. Doing so is the definition of fulfilment as exercising and developing our special trait is equal to the fulfilment of our purpose of existence. In order to reach this fulfilment, people are increasingly trying to become richer, which also led to the accumulation of economic means gaining massive importance in contemporary economies. Because of that, it is only natural that expanding financial means gradually moved in the focus of people's behaviour, eventually becoming an end in itself which is a clear case of goal displacement – even though the starting point of this development was centred around noble intentions. With excessive means, economically stronger actors can create situations in which weaker economic actors practically work on the fulfilment of another person and are unable to develop their own special trait; either because there is no time or energy, or because the person has adopted the goals of the economically stronger actor. Such a situation emerged because economic conduct was not subject to sufficient normative and legal guidance that keeps it in line with the goals of Devletism. Such a goal displacement is caused by a lacking awareness of the purpose of existence.

A free market economy enables dynamics to freely unfold, but the reason why money has become a desirable goal is that the political systems of our day are unaware of the aim of societal progression. The individual is not to blame for her pursuit of money but rather the structures that make her perceive money as an attractive thing to pursue. Whenever societies develop ill tendencies, the underlying structures are to be blamed for it as humans merely act naturally within the boundaries of the material and normative structures of the society. Therefore, politics is necessary to craft suitable structures and constantly improve them, for societies to naturally adopt progressive behaviour.

Devletism constitutes a holistic approach to personal and societal progress, basically forming the bridge between those two. Individual progress is key in achieving societal progress, but it is only a truly societal development if the whole society is able to engage in genuine knowledge production. In the light of our discussion of economic systems, contemporary political systems will favour a fully free market economy. The reason for that is the centrality of personal comfort. Unlike Devletism, most political systems do not encompass a well-structured view around the purpose of our existence. Therefore, contemporary political systems are merely keen on creating comfort for their citizens. Comfort is inherently grounded in material stability and even more so in luxury. Accordingly, political success is often assessed in terms of providing citizens with just that. Making those two aspects widely accessible to a society can only be done by economic means, which is why economies have become so important today within statesmanship. The fully free market economy provides an environment where producers can dynamically react to the demand for luxury. Because demand for luxury is inexhaustible, consumption of luxury goods will constantly increase as long as the production expands. Certainly, the economic volume grows in such a situation, given that the political system provides the necessary preconditions for the consumption of luxury goods, such as avoidance of war or ensuring that the average worker earns above the subsistence level. However, in such an environment, the economically stronger actors, who we have discussed just before, will use their financial capabilities to spur the demand for consumption, in order to extract maximum economic value from the consumers. With increasing growth, the marginal return on investment decreases. This means that bigger companies will have to invest comparatively more into their growth, to sustain the same growth rates as smaller companies.

At some point, the cost of investment will be higher than the return of that investment as the company will approach its natural growth limit. Since the fully free market economy has a displaced goal of ever-increasing wealth, comfort and luxury and does not have normative guidance of business conduct, corporations will seek to expand the natural limits of their growth which means that the environment, within which they operate, needs to be artificially altered. Through advertising, brand-building, expansion in vast areas of the economy and other strategies, these economic actors constantly find new ways to increase the rate of consumption, to sustain high growth rates of their businesses when all other investment opportunities, which can be applied internally and produce a positive return, are exhausted. The company can then maintain this output level and grow at a rate parallel to the changes of the economic environment it is altering.

Next to utilising the greatly stretched boundaries of the free market economy, businesses are also keen on finding ways to reduce their cost by means of ethically unacceptable methods. Tax evasion, underpaying employees, use of environmentally harmful resources, exerting political and legal pressure in economically weak but resource-rich regions and many other practices have become common. Unfortunately, with increasing economic power, these economic actors are also increasingly favoured by the legal and political system, due to their structural importance within the construct of ever-increasing consumption and production.[45] Because a fully free market economy creates more favourable conditions for economically strong actors, a greater volume of the overall economy means more favourable conditions for nations on the international plane. This is why states tend to bend legal rules for powerful economic actors, in order to maintain and increase their political power internationally through the volume of their economic output.

The key difference between economic power of private economic actors within a nation and the economic power between nations is the drive behind the behaviour – or in other words: the purpose. Due to the structure of contemporary political, and consequently also economic, systems, the purpose of economic conduct has become the increase of comfort through consumption and luxury which are purposes not aligned with the

---

[45] Not only can those actors afford better legal protection but with a certain size the public actors begin to question the cost-benefit relationship of punishing large economic actors for the sake of fairness. With their significant tax contributions, great numbers of employees and potentially ownership of strategically or structurally important assets, like banks or producers of military technology, contemporary systems tend to accept legal breaches of those asset holders.

principles of genuine knowledge production as they do not help to better understand the objective truth. States, on the other hand, are still mainly concerned with securing the survival of their nation and generating wealth and prosperity. They often do not do this in the name of genuine knowledge production and sometimes focus too much on the aspect of wealth and comfort, as it was discussed above, but the extent to which this is happening is still often more aligned with genuine knowledge production as these are also enabling factors.

For both sides, private and public, however, the same problem persists to some extent: the lack of purpose. It is only a matter of time until politics, too, becomes dysfunctional, due to this lack purpose because at some point they will have shifted their focus exclusively to the expansion of consumption and luxury, which is arguably already the case in some nations. Therefore, the economy within a devletist system is one with purpose. Because it is such a meaningful purpose, economic growth will reach unprecedented rates and the quality will be much higher. Today, economies grow at a high pace, but the quality of economic output decreases immensely. The growth is driven by increased consumer spending on luxury goods and brands as well as a high replacement rate of products. By doing so, citizens will have fewer financial means to allocate to knowledge-producing activities, while not having any added value for the extra money spent.

Further, the entertainment industry has become one of the most powerful industries in the contemporary economy but even more so in political terms. With an increasing population focusing on material comfort, the demand for value-creation has decreased greatly. Replaced is this drive for value-creation with entertainment, mainly in digital form. In such an environment of comfort, the demand for easily processable formats is increasing which the entertainment industries readily serve. This has a detrimental effect because comfort then becomes a habit and further creates barriers to knowledge production as this is a process which requires a great amount of energy and cognitive input. Although with the invention of the internet we can basically access most of the information mankind has accumulated throughout countless millennia, the entertainment industry thrives off the communication of cognitively non-demanding content. On the political side, this leads to the misperception that the best form of political systems is one that adds to the personal comfort, ideally with simultaneously decreasing effort that is required to obtain this comfort. This decadent mentality guarantees the demise of any society but is in the short run an attractive tool of manipulative politics. If we add this factor to the disadvantages of contemporary economic systems, the necessity to shift to the devletist economy becomes even clearer.

Another indicator of the low quality of contemporary economies is the misalignment of production principles. When we adopt a devletist lens, we would naturally expect that every person is trying her best she can to produce the best possible outcome in any activity she engages in. This holds especially true for people who have found their special trait and work to produce real-world outcomes with it. Within devletist systems, it is aimed at increasing the number of those people. However, even people who have not yet found their special trait or are unable to pursue its development will try to maximise the quality of any outcome of their actions, due to the improved education system and all the other political structures that are designed in a way that makes success within the devletist system only possible if we adopt such a mentality. This certainly translates into the economy.

From this, we would expect all producers to produce goods to their highest possible quality, with the most efficient use of sustainable resources. In the devletist economy, this is the core notion that the structures need to be built around. Everything in the economy must be produced to the highest possible quality and in the most efficient way. Today, producers often design products for a limited period of trouble-free use, in order to maintain a high replacement rate of the products. With an artificially shortened replacement rate, producers aim at continuous consumption, though at the expense of the environment and the financial stability of the consumers.[46] For example, if a useful product, such as a light bulb, needs to be replaced every three years, the consumption rate is artificially increased. Then, if the true lifespan of a light bulb – produced with the best and most sustainable materials in the most efficient way, utilising the most advanced technology – is 50 years, which excursively is easily realisable, then the economic output that the artificially sustained consumption rate produced is not reflecting the true economic performance of the nation.[47]

Certainly, the example of the light bulb is only a small one, but when we apply this idea to all products, then we will quickly realise that output of contemporary economies is not truly reflective of the economic performance. We can say that the fully free market economy is producing bubble economies. In combination with the corporations' attempts to alter the economic environment through promoting valueless content and consumption of luxury goods and brands, the increased replacement rate is another factor that also lessens the utility of money as a useful indicator of the true value of goods and services, as it was indicated earlier.

---

[46] Many companies, especially manufacturers of electronic devices, apply mechanisms to reduce the product quality of older products, in order to create new buying incentives for customers.

[47] The longest lasting light bulb burns over 120 years. *The Centennial Light of Livermore* burns since 1901.

Money can be useful when the right normative framework is providing the necessary structure in form of a sound economic system. However, if economic conduct is moved away from the principles of quality and utilisation in the light of the societal purpose, money, too, becomes an artificially altered factor that merely represents the price of a good or service but not the true value. On the other hand, money within the devletist economy reflects the true value of goods and services, because the economy is structured to achieve our purpose of existence and money can, to a certain degree, be viewed as the quantification of that value.

Chapter XIX

Principles and Policies in the Devletist Economy and Finance

After this long critique of contemporary economies, it is now time to turn to the main principles of the devletist economy. It was already outlined that the economy within devletist systems is designed to enable all citizens to engage in genuine knowledge production and translate their efforts into real-world outcomes. Therefore, it is important that citizens can monetise their efforts, in order to provide for their material needs. The only way, in which this can be done, is to create a demand for a wide range of goods and services that are aligned with our purpose of existence. Today, archaeologists, professors, painters and many other professions are greatly underpaid, even though their works are essential in our endeavour to improve our understanding of the world. Because these works are not contributing to the comfort of the masses, the readiness to pay for those services is low – there is insufficient demand. On the other hand, we can look at a bar owner or a producer of telephone cases who will, with the right business model, earn significantly more money and sustain a seemingly better lifestyle.

However, these activities seldom add to the progression of the society – if ever. This does not mean that these services and goods should be prohibited, but the monetary reward of providing them should be reflective of their influence on societal progression. Again, money is an important tool to quantify the value but only if the economic direction is rectified.

Within devletist systems one important step towards the rectification of demand is done at the educational level. The previously outlined structures, help to properly educate citizens to pursue goals and ambitions that reach far beyond the plain wish to live in material comfort. Further, because the system is designed in a way that helps people develop an interest in a number of topics and increase attentiveness to the purpose of genuine knowledge production, children inherently grow up with a lower urge to consume as they will rather find comfort in engaging with more purposeful activities.

Moreover, due to this higher level of awareness, the ambitious education and rectified set of values, the readiness to overpay for goods and services with lesser value decreases, too. Someone who has found her special trait, continuously develops it and makes progress in translating it into meaningful outcomes will not be ready to spend her money, which she has laboriously earned, on, for instance, designer-branded clothes, which are, in essence, of the same quality as unbranded textiles. It does not make economic sense because it would mean that she is exchanging the valuable time of hers for goods that are artificially priced above their true value.

Further, she will not have the urge to impress her social environment with such clothes or other luxury items. However, she would rather spend her laboriously earned money on goods and services that she feels are worthy in terms of her time and energy spent on obtaining it. For example, she will rather spend it on vacations, books, paintings, her hobbies, investments or other activities that have more value than plain consumption. The better the education system functions, the more people will behave this way economically. The more people behave like that economically, the more expensive valuable goods and services will become, while the prices for less valuable goods and services will decrease. An important development takes place here because the prices will start to properly reflect the hierarchy of value between the goods and services. From a societal perspective, this is very desirable because then the aforementioned archaeologists, professors, painters and other professions will gain, through economic power, more prestige within society as the monetary value reflects that their work is more demanded.

Next to the utilisation of education to rectify the ill-structured hierarchy of goods and services, there are also some legal tools that politics can utilise to craft more meaningful economies. In an attempt to curb overpricing, businesses should be prohibited to charge a profit margin of more than 20%. This means that after calculating all costs of production of goods or providing a service, businesses should only be allowed to charge 20% more as pure profit. By doing so, it is prevented that businesses create monopolistic structures and artificial prices for their goods and services. Also, there is no normative argument that could reasonably defend profit margins above 20%. Producers might argue that if the buyer might be willing to pay more, but in such a case, worker pay can be increased, instead of adding the extra price to the profits of the producer.

This leads to the next point: labour costs. The cost of human capital needs to be at a fair level, which not only means that a minimum wage needs to be an inherent part of an economy, but worker pay should also be in harmony with management pay, meaning that the discrepancy between top-level management and the average worker should not be excessive, or at least be warranted. There is no blueprint here because economic conduct can be very different as well as the cultural framework within which it happens. However, if we were to solely apply a profit margin cap of 20%, businesses would be inclined to reduce human capital cost at the lower salary levels, to remain competitive. Rather, it is desirable that businesses retain high levels of pay for all employees, while staying close to the respective profit margin cap.

Another structural aspect of the devletist economy is that goods are produced with the lowest possible replacement rate. Returning to the light bulb example, manufacturers should aim at producing the longest-lasting light bulb. In the devletist economy, the purpose of business is that people can use the products and not to enrich the manufacturer because the organisational interest of the business must not compromise societal progression. If all goods are produced in a more sustainable way, more money is available for more meaningful activities. In other words, citizens should use their money for more useful things than constantly replacing their light bulbs.

Again, this is a very simple example, but if we think about all the cheaply produced textiles, electronic devices, toys and many other goods, a lot of money is wasted just because businesses want to retain high rates of returning customers. With the requirement to make products lasting longer, businesses are forced to use materials of the highest quality. This high-quality approach will also have subliminal effects on people's behaviour and productivity. It creates well-being and positivity, which influences behaviour on all levels. We can apply this to the field of urban planning, in order to illustrate this point more clearly. A clean city with high-quality housing, proper roads and beautiful parks will create a positive atmosphere and foster well-being, while cheap and dirty neighbourhoods tend to promote discomfort, unproductivity and often even violence and crime. This point will receive special attention in the later course of this work.

Linked to the requirement of low replacement rates, the production of goods also needs to happen in the most efficient and environmentally sustainable way. This means that the production processes should leave the lowest possible effect on the ecosystem; especially, wildlife needs to be protected at all costs. All aspects of the supply and production chain need to be optimised to reduce intervention in the natural functioning of the ecosystem. Beginning from the energy supply, all the way to avoiding deforestation and making the meat industry subject to strict rules, businesses are responsible for keeping the effects on the ecosystem at the lowest. Now, the attentive reader will quickly identify a conflict between the use of high-quality materials and sustainable production of the goods. Here, lowering the negative effects on the ecosystem should have priority over the use of high-quality materials. For instance, the production of jackets can be looked at to illustrate this point. Fur or down jackets are best to protect its wearer from the cold. However, their production constitutes a harsh intervention in the functioning of the nature which must be avoided at all costs. Here, the jacket producer will be forced to use materials that are less burdensome on the environment.

Luckily, this has an innovative effect on the structure of the business. Because it would be legally obliged to increase the quality of the product without burdening the ecosystem, the business is forced to develop technologies that combine these two aspects. Through the normative guidance of these two devletist economic principles, the business is forced to engage in genuine knowledge production – something that fully free market economies are unable to do. Under the free market economy, the business would solely develop in a way that would improve its profits, disregarding the effects on the environment or the utility of the consumer. In the devletist economy, businesses have normative boundaries which force them to advance technologically, in order to stay competitive. Rather than allocating resources or setting research and development requirements, devletist economies set simple normative rules that need to be followed. Economic conduct is then bound to develop in the desired direction itself, which is much more effective than state-controlled economic conduct. Just like humans are not to be blamed for misconduct because the system guides them to do so, the power of structures can be applied to the economy as well, in order to further our cause of existence.

Next, there are also social aspects that need consideration in the production and supply chains of businesses. Exploitation of workers and child labour must be prohibited. Regarding exploitation, it was previously outlined that a minimum wage should be applied and that salary discrepancies between management and the average employee should be reduced in an acceptable way. Another aspect that the devletist economy needs to incorporate is the reduction of working hours. Contemporary economic systems are built around the standard of the forty-hours work week. However, it is important to bear in mind that the purpose of existence is not consumption. Therefore, the economic system needs to create room for people to pursue their passions, not only at their respective workplaces but in private, too. Naturally, this requires time and energy. The standard work week should be around thirty hours. In this way, it can be ensured that citizens have enough time to develop themselves. It should also not be forgotten that the political system requires its citizens to constantly engage in politics because of the voting structure. Ambitious citizens will have a hard time to expand their political knowledge and attend the examinations to acquire voting rights when they are overly occupied by their work. Further, the reduced working hours will require businesses to employ more people, in order to uphold their efficient production levels, which reduces unemployment. Paired with the minimum wage requirement, however, the production costs of businesses will increase, driving up prices of goods and services. This way, consumers will make increasingly conscious consumption decisions, due to increasing prices. All in all, these guidelines will help contemporary economies to get rid of excess consumption, rectify the normative perception of economic conduct, increase quality of economic output and enable people to work on their personal fulfilment. It can be summarised that the devletist economy aims at operating at its true potential and not at its artificial one. In the transition period from the current systems, this will mean a great reduction in the absolute value of economies. The gross domestic products of current economies could be halved, but the growth that will follow from that point on will be structurally stable, ecologically and economically sustainable and productive in the light of true societal progress.

All the above also aid the growth and stability of the financial systems of economies. Because businesses will be obliged to operate according to the rectified framework of norms and values, the downside risk of business conduct is greatly reduced. With it, the investment landscape will become more stable and offer more potential for all investors to expand their wealth. Of course, the upside risk can also be negatively affected, due to the profit margin cap. However, this does not mean that financial market gains are completely compromised because the valuation of companies is still subject to the free fluctuation of money. Therefore, a company's stock price development can exceed its maximum of 20% growth of revenues. This is even more likely to be the case because companies will need to try more actively to attract funding in the capital market. One aspect that facilitates the search for more funding is the reduced downside risk of publicly traded companies. Since companies' operations need to adhere to the devletist guidelines, they are more likely to survive and succeed in the long run. This certainly creates incentives to make companies publicly tradeable, because that way, greater financing can be ensured.

Hence, the financial markets gain massive importance in the devletist economy. For one, more companies will be publicly traded. Secondly, more citizens will invest in the economy at higher levels of stability and receive greater financial gains. Through this increased flow of financing, both sides of the investment gain, while innovation and economic expansion are accelerated. With this expansion of the financing sector, the rate of innovation will be increased, as it is the only way corporations can gain advantage over their competitors in search for funding. In short, the volume of business conduct will play a secondary role in the quality of business conduct. Another effect that comes with the greater stability of financial returns is that private investors will have more financial means to allocate to their personal development, which amplifies societal progress once more. Summarising, it can be stated that the normative guidelines within the devletist economy vastly reduce downside risk of business conduct, due to the rectification of economic goals. It further helps to purify the absolute value of economies which currently operate artificially above their true potential, a detrimental situation in the long run and, therefore, posing the risk of systemic failure.

Chapter XX

Public Income and Expenditure

It is debatable to what extent public income and expenditure can be categorised under the policy area of the economy, but since it is defined as the monetised exchanges within a nation, the topics of taxation and public expenditure should be discussed in this concluding chapter on the economy within the devletist state. The previous chapter outlined the principles that private business conduct should adhere to, but there are also many public institutions that the state needs to function properly. Further, and we have not yet touched upon that topic, there are also welfare structures that need to be financed. We cannot but to accept that a society is only functionable as long as there is a state authority that provides for its key structures. Taxation, therefore, is a central topic. Within this topic, however, the factor of culture-based policymaking carries a lot of weight. The reason for that is that societies are very different in terms of the acceptance of state intervention.

Whereas some societies favour a more comprehensive role of the state in matters of social policies, for instance, other societies are less acceptant of such intervention. With it, the structure of taxation and use of those means are influenced. Further, it needs to be pointed out that taxation can have a strongly redistributing dimension. We can think about socially oriented states that are currently laying a greater tax burden on higher income households, to flatten out some social and economic discrepancies between the groups of different income levels. In different cultural contexts, this should naturally vary. Where the economic discrepancy within a society is low, there is no need for higher burdens on certain groups. If we also think about a political system where people can equally well engage in genuine knowledge production despite greater economic discrepancies, there is no need for different taxation levels, either. However, if the economic discrepancies between the groups are so great that they endanger social cohesion and significantly favour the economically advanced groups, a redistributive tax policy could help to close the income gap between the groups.[48]

Nonetheless, there are some general principles that all states can structure this policy around. First and foremost, taxation and social security contributions should in total not exceed one third of a person's or business' income. However, the rate should also not be lower than one fifth of a person's or business' income, for them to retain a material argument for political representation. If the contribution to the state is too low, the danger of disconnection between government and citizen increases, due to

---

[48] Due to the technocratic approach, (non-)redistributive tax policies need to be periodically re-evaluated because the economic and social circumstances are constantly changing.

lacking interdependency.[49] Nevertheless, it is important that the income remains mainly in the hands of the person who has earned it. Even if a state is using the taxation income in the most efficient way and offer its citizens the highest possible standard of living, development and security, working people should still have the feeling of earning their income for themselves and not of shouldering the functioning of the state. Like that, citizens will also have more means available to allocate to their personal development. It should also be noted that there are many other state-incurred costs that citizens need to bear. Issuance of passports, value added tax, inheritance tax, issuance of driver's licences and many other costs are often rolled off on the citizen (which should ideally not be the case) and further add to the fact that income taxes (including social security contributions) above one third of the income cannot be justified.

From the state perspective, this amount should also suffice to maintain a smooth functioning of all state institutions and processes. If that is not the case, it might indicate that there are inefficiencies on the side of public expenditure. In the devletist state, the institutions that are financially most burdensome on the treasury are certainly the education ministry, election ministry, urban planning and environment ministries, the military and

---

[49] Beblawi, Hazem. "The Rentier State in the Arab World." *Arab Studies Quarterly* 9, no. 4 (1987): 383–98.

ministry for welfare affairs. As one would expect, the education ministry should ideally receive the largest portion of the household since it is not only central to the devletist state but also offers the greatest return on investment. This leads to a very central principle within the management of public expenditure. Every point of cost should be questioned in the light of its projected return in terms of genuine knowledge production. Thinking about the education ministry, it is quite clear that high teacher pay will correlate with better student performance because teachers are incentivised to put in more effort into their profession. Also, monitoring teacher performance through the relevant institutions within the election ministry will have a high return on investment because it is another cost point that has the effect of future generations becoming cognitively more advanced.

Let us now compare these aspects with expenditure on matters related to the police force. There is no doubt that the police force needs to be somewhat well-equipped, in order to ensure domestic security. However, it is not necessary for it to upgrade its equipment frequently. For example, police cars that are ten to fifteen years old will, in general, be sufficient for officers to properly do their job. The added value of replacing the police cars every four years, for instance, is negligible. Moreover, the work of the police force has less potential to add to a society's production of genuine knowledge and a rather passive role within the state functioning. If we extend the argument even further, it needs to be acknowledged that the expenditure required for the police force will also be reduced with increased spending on education, for example, because within a well-educated society criminality is less likely to flourish. The same holds true for economic prosperity, because if many citizens can sustain a materially and immaterially fulfilling lifestyle, the inclination towards crime is reduced. Public expenditure, therefore, needs to be attentive to its potential and actual returns.

An aspect which follows from this argument is that the calculation of returns on investment will also influence the timing of replacing and renewing previous investments. A road that is not heavily used has little economic or infrastructural value and does not need to be renewed as frequently as a road that fulfils one or more of the enlisted factors. However, if there is a road that has, for example, great economic value, the renewing process should happen not only frequently but also in a quick fashion. Here, the construction company should double or even triple the number of workers, to reduce the time the road has limited usage as much as possible.

The invested capital has greater value because it reduces the transaction cost during the renewal and enables a quicker return to the normal rate of traffic. This concept can also be applied to all other areas of public expenditure. The government (depending on the mode of governance, this can also be the local or provincial government) is responsible for prioritising points of cost in the light of their projected returns. Of course, not all aspects within a state can be strongly linked to knowledge production but this fact alone would make the relevant area a less valuable point of cost, compared to other areas that are much more intertwined with genuine knowledge production.

Now, there will not be a single scholar or politician who would defend the inefficient use of monetary means of the state, and many would agree that the funds should be allocated in a way that produce the greatest return on investment. What sounds easy in theory can be subject to great difficulties in practise. Often, decisions on the use of financial resources are subject to complicated decision-making procedures and lack proper analysis, due to insufficient human resources to shoulder the vast amount of investment analysis that is required. That alone leads to inefficiencies in spending, but also the selection of contractors is a major aspect that drains the treasury. Due to complex bureaucratic structures that make decisions on spending already difficult, the funds are often quickly allocated to the first best contractor. Nepotism is also very common in this area of public expenditure. Knowing about their strategic advantage, contractors often increase their prices. Other than private spending, public spending is less attentive to financial efficiency because the civil servants who manage the process are ultimately not managing their personal funds but those of "others". This leads to a lax use of funds – either intentionally or unintentionally. In order to counteract this, a high degree of integrity on the side of the civil servants is required. Surely, this can be difficult to achieve in practise, too. Therefore, the structures and processes need to be adapted. In general, public spending that involves contractors needs to be subject to greater competition and transparency because then more efficient rates can be achieved. One way to increase the competition between contractors is to publish all current projects that are aimed to involve contractors as well as all past projects and the final amounts that were paid. This not only creates the incentives for businesses to constantly monitor state-funded projects and seek for business opportunities but also increases transparency. Here, transparency has also a positive effect on public accountability as the public spending procedures are subject to greater scrutiny by the general public.

Next to public expenditure related to work with contractors, all other points of cost should be made publicly available. Beginning with the dining expenses and cars of government officials, all the way to investments in infrastructure, there needs to be a high degree of transparency, including the reduction of barriers to access the relevant information. Only the disclosures of public expenditure that could endanger national security should be exempt from this requirement. Research spending on new military technologies would, for instance, fall under this category.

However, the idea behind the transparency requirement is clear: higher accountability through public scrutiny. This point is also less subject to culture-based policymaking as taxpayers have an inherent right to monitor the expenses of the state since they are the main source of financing public expenditure, but even more important is the fact that states exist for the citizens and not the other way around. However, if the quality of policy output is high, citizens are unlikely to voice dissatisfaction with the tax structure and expenditure. Transparency is certainly an important aspect of such high-quality policy output.

Chapter XXI

International Relations in a Devletist World

Devletism is structured around the notion of the state. The nation state has dominated political thinking for much of the past centuries and, for the time being, remains the most feasible concept of structuring politics. This does not always have to be the case. Earlier, the concept of supranational governance was also included in the modes of government. It could well be that in the following centuries, politics will gradually see the emergence of supranational structures and potentially even a single world state. Contrary, it could also develop into a more fractioned political landscape with smaller political entities. However, Devletism does not lose significance in either case because it assumes that there will be at least one state or state-like entity, which then can be designed in a devletist way. With the exception of a cosmopolitan world order, in which there is only one single global state, there will be a part of politics that is concerned with the relations between states;[50] and even within such a hypothetical cosmopolitan state, we can reasonably expect that this policy area is concerned with the management of

---

[50] Being derived from the Greek word *kosmopolites*, meaning *citizen of the world*, the idea can be first traced back to Diogenes the Cynic (Diogenes Laertius, Book VI, 63).

relations between all the societies within the state as they are inherently different. Hence, *foreign affairs*, or *international relations*, is an integral part of any political system and the next policy area that is examined here (within a cosmopolitan state, it might be called intersocietal relations). Further, the military is also included in this policy area because the military is most often utilised in transnational conduct of a state. The most frequent domestic use of military forces is at the borders of a nation, which has an inherent transnational purpose.[51]

Under foreign affairs, all interactions between two or more states are to be understood. There are many reasons why interaction between states is not only unavoidable but also desired in most cases. For one, there is a normative argument for it because citizens of different nations frequently travel to other nations and this should, in principle, not be prohibited because in the strictest sense territorial boundaries were artificially constructed by humans. Although our nature requires governance and this governance is done effectively within designated boundaries of the respective societies, our planet should be relatively freely accessible, if we were to look at it from a perspective that is isolated from political considerations. Although we have already seen that social cohesion is also an

---

[51] This holds true in times of peace. During war, it should be clear that militaries engage in transterritorial conduct.

important aspect of proper state functioning, the main idea remains that the movement of people across borders is an inherent part of our behaviour and right as organisms of this planet.

Another factor that adds to the international conduct is concerned with the resources of the respective nations. Not all resources are equally available within all state territories, although some resources are indispensable for the survival and development of societies. The most important resource is water. There are water abundant regions in the world, while other nations have struggles to meet their society's demand for water. Procuring essential, as well as non-essential, resources will force nations to cooperate and enter into diplomatic, economic or even military conduct. Moreover, national territorial boundaries are often treated as undisputable and fixed. However, in many regions there are great disagreements between societies about the definition of territorial boundaries. States or societal leaders are then leading the resolution with their respective counterparts – either through non-violent means of diplomacy or through the use of economic or military coercion. In all of these cases, there is interaction between at least two societies. It is important to acknowledge that foreign affairs also include transnational interaction with non-state actors, such as international organisations, military groups or even whole societies which do not have a sovereign state, let alone a defined territory.[52] So, there is a wide range of activities that fall under the umbrella of foreign affairs and the efficient and effective structure and management of this policy field plays an important role in the nation's endeavour to develop.

Of course, we have a situation of continuous interaction between those societal entities, but nonetheless there is much value in approaching this chapter with a layered approach. This means that there is a hierarchical prioritisation between the different aspects of foreign affairs, which can, therefore, be described as stages of foreign policy. There are 7 main stages of foreign policy and an optional 8th stage, which requires attention on a situational basis.

At the most basic level, a society, aspiring to become a state, needs to establish territorial boundaries. In exceptional cases, such as island societies, this is rather easy if the island is inhabited by one society only. There is little that speaks against the establishment of a nation here and societies that did not naturally originate from that island should respect the exclusiveness of that territory. More common, however, is the

---

[52] We must acknowledge that these actors, too, have the capacity to draw significant attention and power towards them. Accordingly, the conduct with these actors, regardless of positive or negative nature, cannot be disregarded as a part of international relations.

establishment of nations on great land masses that are inhabited by many different societies, of which many also aspire the establishment of an exclusive societal order by means of politics. Where the living spaces of those societies are relatively clearly distinct, those societies will form their states within the territory of their historic development. While the exclusiveness of core territories is usually not very often subject to debate, the border territories often cause potential points of friction because it cannot be clearly defined where one society ends and the other begins, due to our inherent tendency to move as well as geostrategic and resource-oriented interests. In *the state-formation stage*, foreign affairs are concerned with defining, establishing and defending territorial boundaries by military means.

Without defining the living space, there will always be ambiguity within those territories over how societal conduct is organised, leading not only to inefficiencies on the side of policymaking but also to conflict, hindering progress altogether. It is important that such a military establishing process is reduced to the minimum of territorial expansion and needs to be justifiable in terms of the respective society's cultural history within that claimed territory. For example, the borders of Germany in its current form can be fully justified in terms of the Germans past within that territory. Their ethnicity originated there, inhabited it for a long period and also successfully administered it. Surely, it is debatable whether some German-inhabited territories of France, Poland, the Netherlands and Czech Republic could also fall under German sovereignty, due to their past. However, this question would not arise when we talk about the core lands of the Germans stretching from Hamburg over Hanover to Stuttgart or Munich. There is also no debate about whether Germans should have any sovereignty rights in former colonies, such as Namibia, which they clearly have not.

Through military conduct, the current borders of Germany and many other states were formed and although the situation in this specific case seems to have ended up in an agreeable territorial solution, this is not the case everywhere. Some states are still struggling between each other to define the borders between their states. Giving contemporary examples, Russia and Ukraine continue to have unclarities about their borders, as well as Azerbaycan and Armenia. With such unclarities still being existent, we are turning to the second stage of foreign policy: defending territorial borders. Germany would not be able to exist in its current form if it was not able to defend its borders. Moreover, Azerbaycan will not reach full policy efficiency if it is not able to defend its borders against Armenia and the other way around.

Therefore, after having established a territorial frame for the own state, a society needs to defend these borders for a long time, in order to create an international acceptance of those borders. This is *the second stage of foreign policy*. When Russia annexed the Crimean Peninsula, many states opposed the recognition of that territory as Russian.[53] Today, there is little debate whether Crimea is to be counted as Russian or not, although formally it is still not recognised as such by some states. However, if Russia was to lower its military presence at the Crimean borders, effectively ceasing to defend it, there will be immediate action from Ukraine because not enough time has passed for a general acceptance to solidify. In a couple of centuries, there will be little need to further defend this territory, due to the acceptance that this territory is now Russian. Certainly, this would not be the case if the ethnic composition was not mostly Russian.[54] Thinking about Israel, this state has been defending its borders for almost a century now but will have to continue to do so because the ethnic composition of the territory is not sufficiently homogeneous, while a heated conflict over those lands persists. This is also the reason why Israel is trying to increase the ethnic homogeneity of its society.[55] Only then, the state can claim full

---

[53] United Nations, General Assembly, *Resolution 68/262*, April 1, 2014.

[54] The ethnic composition of Crimea is widely disputed as the true answer to this question would determine the political future of the peninsula. While originally being home to Crimean Tatars, a Turkic ethnicity, its long history with the Soviet Union and the results of the 2014 referendum, which asked Crimeans whether they would support territorial belongingness to Russia, indicate that the demographics shifted to a majority of Russians.

[55] Since 1967, Israel is pursuing a settlement policy into Arab territories, aiming at gradual shift of power through stronger presence in those territories.

sovereignty over the territory by defending it for some centuries more. The scenario is relatively simple: if the Palestinian minority in Israel is very small, the state will only have to defend it for one or two more centuries. By that time, the global community, including the Palestinians, will be used to this situation and Israel's sovereignty over the lands will be accepted. If Palestinians remain a considerably strong minority, even some millennia will not suffice to create acceptance of the Israeli state, thus, requiring constant defence of the territory.

Somewhat overlapping with the second stage, but nonetheless considered as the next distinct stage of foreign policy, is the building of legitimacy. This aspect is tied to the acceptance of the own state by the global state community. Legitimacy, however, goes beyond mere acceptance as it is the requirement for the equal legal treatment of the state among all the other states. When a state is not able to establish distinct boundaries and defend those, it cannot expect to be treated as a legitimate state. Not all states will automatically accept the formation of a new state and recognise it as such and sometimes there is only partial recognition of this new state. Often, state legitimacy is then reduced to the core territories, while the legal status of the disputed areas remains somewhat in the dark. Again, the Palestinians serve as a suitable example of a society with a legitimacy problem. Due to the ongoing conflict with Israel, where both parties are unable to clearly defend the claimed borders, the international community has ambiguous stances towards those regions, while the core regions of the two parties are rather unambiguously acknowledged as existing and subject to a certain degree of sovereignty by the respective party.

The same holds true for the disputed regions between Azerbaycan and Armenia. Probably no state would argue about the belongingness of Baku to Azerbaycan as well as the belongingness of Yerevan to Armenia. However, due to the lack of continued sovereignty in the disputed areas, the international community's stance on their legitimacy naturally varies. It might seem like *the third stage of foreign policy*, namely legitimacy-building, is an exclusively military facet of foreign policy, yet it should rather be seen as a diplomatic stage. Surely, its precondition is military action but at the core of legitimacy-building lays diplomatic conduct. This is achieved through seeking support in the international community. Ideally, stronger nations defend the territorial claims of the nation with territorial disputes. If the Palestinians did not resort to diplomatic means to defend their claimed territory, they would have been forced to give up their aspirations of an own state a long time ago.

The Jews, in turn, would have had a much more difficult time conquering Palestine if they did not engage in legitimacy-building diplomatic conduct in England long before the collapse of the Ottoman Empire. In this case, the Jews successfully lobbied for the power transfer from the British to their own people, eventually establishing Israel.[56] Another way to achieve legitimacy through diplomacy is to raise the stakes of stronger nations in the potential solidification of the own state. In the founding process of the Turkish Republic, the Treaty of Moscow played an important role. Even though Türkiye was not a recognised state at that time (1921), Russia, on the verge of establishing the Soviet Union, signed a treaty with Türkiye. With it, it recognised the existence of Türkiye as a state as well as established its identity as the Soviet Union through an international legal agreement. Thus, Russia, as a considerably stronger actor than Türkiye at that time, had a heightened interest in Türkiye's recognition because she was a first actor that would reliably recognise its aspired borders. If Türkiye was not to be recognised internationally, the Treaty of Moscow would have been null and void. Accordingly, diplomatic means are the main channel to generate legitimacy as they are also longer-lasting than military means since coercion is more difficult to sustain in the long-run than persuasion or conviction.

After establishing its borders, defending them and gaining widespread international legitimacy, a state should seek to

---

[56] Şentürk, Emre. "White, White World – A Racial Perspective on the Founding of Israel." Bachelor's thesis. University of Groningen, 2017.

improve its bi- and multilateral ties with other nations, at *the fourth stage of foreign policy*. Doing so creates a more favourable environment for foreign policymaking. Sustaining positive relations with other nations will increase the degree of readiness to enter compromise, which, in turn, will lead to better policy outcomes in terms of their own national interests. Having friendly relations with nations will create a certain degree of trust and positivity, leading to more effective cooperation and less friction. It is important to note that this must happen in an unbiased way because every positive connection to another nation will increase the potential of the own nation's potential and actual development. The potential resources of development are increased, due to a more fertile environment. Where possible, antagonism should be avoided. Of course, this is difficult, due to ideological or sometimes even religious motives, but since the devletist state is a technocratic one, these considerations will only play a role in the most exceptional cases. Religious considerations should in no case play a role within devletist policymaking if it leads to antagonism. It can influence culture-based policymaking (also internationally) but only in light of positive political agendas. For example, if certain religious customs are part of the cultural core of a society, they ought to be embraced. However, adopting an antagonistic stance towards another nation on the grounds of religious differences conflicts with the ideas of technocratic devletist governance.

Based on this positive foreign policy environment, *the fifth stage of foreign policy* is concerned with fostering economic cooperation with other nations. This should also be approached technocratically and in an unbiased way, in order to extract maximum economic value from transnational economic conduct. Grounded in the same assumption that economic ties increase the potential of a nation's course of development, it is important that a nation seeks to ever-improve the conditions of economic conduct. Under such ambitions fall the diplomatic means of reducing trade barriers, customs, raising production standards and crafting more favourable frameworks for the establishment of transnational business. Also, foreign direct investment plays a great value-generating role for all involved parties. Certainly, we have seen in the past that economic means were used to expand political power within another state.[57] However, if the state-formation processes were based on devletist principles of territorial exclusiveness stemming from ethnic history within a territory, there is little reason for other states to pursue such expansionist policies. Because Devletism is closely built around a healthy understanding of the own nation and its place in the world, devletist states will also have heightened respect towards

---

[57] Not only was economic influence exercised through the "back door", as it is usually done, but the USA even laid the basis for all kinds of intervention in the affairs of Latin American states by articulating the *Roosevelt Corollary*.

other nations. Economic conduct, in the end, returns to what it is in essence: a technocratic policy field. So, a nation should not shy away from seeking new investment and cooperation opportunities with other nations and should actively seek to massively expand efforts to increase and improve international economic ties.

At *the sixth stage of foreign policy*, the matters become less material in their nature but begin to increasingly include normative elements, too. At this stage, states should seek to foster cooperation on problems that transcend their national boundaries. The most prominent problem would be environmental protection. Sea and air pollution, deforestation and the protection of wildlife are aspects that are not merely confined to territorial boundaries, which means that they require international cooperation, in order to be properly dealt with. Channelling material and immaterial resources and competences will lead to more effective and efficient outcomes. Therefore, states need to actively seek cooperation in transnational policy fields, such as the previously mentioned one. But it is not only the environment that requires international cooperation. Public health, education, infrastructure, the internet, judiciary and resource management are all aspects that can be greatly improved through cooperation – sometimes such cooperation is even inevitable. Here, states can build on their improved diplomatic ties as well as on their extensive economic cooperation. Using such a basis, potential points of friction will be reduced and ideally eliminated before general policy cooperation in those areas is extended.

Having dealt with those aspects, states should then seek to foster intercultural exchange on *the seventh and last mandatory stage of devletist foreign policymaking*. With all the material aspects of policymaking off the table, nations can now turn to increase their development potential yet again through learning from other nations. Every nation is unique. Due to their unique history and ethnic properties, societies have inherently developed certain strong points, while other points remain comparatively weak. This special trait of societies, their culture, is the most precious resource of a nation. The aggregate of all cultures forms an almost inexhaustible pool of knowledge and potential for development. Nations should seek to share their knowledge resources, in order to add to the global advancement of our species. Through fostering educational exchanges, leisure travel, cultural exchange programmes, teaching of different languages at schools and alignment of some social political goals, nations can amplify their development simply by diplomatic means. It should be clear that such an exchange is most effectively achieved when the previous stages of foreign policy have reached a high degree of effective operability. Though the stages can overlap and, to varying degrees, be built up simultaneously, reaching a certain degree of operative stability in the previous stages before intensifying the next stage is of much value from an administrative standpoint. Completing all seven mandatory stages will mean that a nation has reached a level of foreign policymaking that complements its domestic politics perfectly. Of course, it is a continuous process and there are sheer endless ways to further improve the workings of foreign policy – especially at the fifth, sixth and seventh stage.

Finally, we then have *a potential eighth stage of foreign policy*. This is a situational stage and best operated at when the previous stages are already functioning efficiently. Here, the defence of other societies' interests is the focus. Unfortunately, not all nations will become devletist at once; and even if they do so, there is no guarantee that they will honour the devletist principles at all times. Nations might still try to expand into the living spaces of other societies. They might still try to expand their cultural influence on other societies. They might still try to economically exploit other societies, thus, infringing a central principle of Devletism. Here, other nations will have to intervene. Surely, the devletist approach goes beyond all those minor goals of material nature, such as pure power, wealth and comfort. The devletist agenda reaches far beyond those aspects because the curiosity about much greater things is the driving notion of it. We can also see the superiority of the devletist goal in the fact that it is not relational. Power, wealth and comfort need points of reference, in order to survive because they are measured against and defined by the power, wealth or comfort of other actors.

In the case of power, more power of one means less power of others. In the case of wealth and comfort, they are measured against the wealth and comfort of others. Genuine knowledge exists independently, does not trigger relational competition and can at most be measured against the internal progress of the respective actor we are looking at, regardless of whether we consider the progress of an individual or a nation. It would, however, be foolish to expect that material interests will not play a role in states' behaviour. There will be states that will still be driven by material motives. Even if a state develops an intrinsic conviction about Devletism, there might be times of egocentric leaders longing for power, pulling a nation into inefficiency and sometimes even misery. Sometimes those leaders might even expand their destructive agenda to other nations and aim to enrich themselves by harming others. Although the key premise of devletist foreign policy is to maintain positive relationships with other nations, devletist nations should also protect other nations from drifting into destructive situations. If, for example, a dictator takes over a nation and prevents her nation from engaging in genuine knowledge production through her policies, other nations should intervene. Also, if a society is subject to repression, persecution or even genocide, other nations are obliged to help. Help can come in the form of diplomacy where especially stronger nations exert diplomatic pressure on or create diplomatic incentives for the aggressor to stop their course of action. Military means must also remain in the repertoire of devletist states to force failing nations to return to a progressive path of policymaking.

However, these aspects are highly problematic from a methodological point of view. Under the name of Devletism, some nations might try to serve their own interests by intervening in other states' domestic affairs. Also, the abovementioned aspects are prone to be turned into a destructive doctrine of devletist intervention. Some nations might radicalise and try to intervene as much as they can whenever the slightest deviation from their own devletist system occurs. But culture-based policymaking is playing a great role under Devletism. Therefore, states cannot merely denounce other states and their practises simply because they deviate from the own structure of policymaking. So, how can we identify true infringement of devletist principles? In the cases of genocide, it is often relatively clear that intervention is warranted and the room for interpretation is little. But what about states with a flawed education system? What about states with a worsening economy? What about a state in which the rulers merely enrich themselves but generally do not harm the population materially or immaterially? What if some rulers are simply incapable and the nation is merely inefficient but not wholly dysfunctional? Would then an intervention not in itself contradict the principles of Devletism in terms of respecting culture-based policymaking?

In such cases, other states should not intervene in the domestic affairs of the state with flawed policymaking – at least not at the military level. It does not mean that these developments should be wholly ignored. Rather, there must be a discussion and diplomatic efforts to rectify the situation, if necessary. Other states should offer financial help and expertise to help such a nation to increase its effectiveness and efficiency again. However, intervening with the slightest sign of bad policy outputs would open the way for another period of colonialism and diplomatic warfare about moral superiority. It is even necessary that every nation lives through these periods of bad policymaking. These are incredibly valuable learning moments for the nation and important additions to the common history, which form and shape the culture of the society. Hence, nations need to find a way to navigate through these times and find a way to incorporate these experiences into a better future. It must be acknowledged that negativity is an integral part of our existence, and this also holds true for our existence on the aggregate level within our societies. In other words, a life without struggle is meaningless. In our personal lives, these periods are rather short for the simple fact that our lifespans are much shorter than those of nations and civilisations. Further, it is then surely a matter of luck to be born into an era of positive progression or not. However, we cannot expect that societies will always experience good times. As long as the bad times are not structurally harmful, or drift into atrocities, societies can cope with somewhat lesser positive periods, even if they happen to persist for some centuries.

It should also be kept in mind that after those less effective and efficient periods, better periods will inevitably follow – given the nation is able to survive. In turn, if a nation is experiencing a particularly successful era, it should be equally kept in mind that this era will eventually come to an end and harder times will inevitably arrive at some point. Managing those periods politically at the domestic level is important. However, when a nation is in danger of drifting into atrocious situations (wars, famine, ethnic cleansing, genocide, natural disasters and so on) other nations are obliged to help. When diplomatic efforts do not suffice to improve the situation, nations should intervene by military means to bridge the situation. Here, intervention must not serve other interests than the interests of the nation that has drifted into a structurally bad situation. Therefore, devletist military intervention in the light of the eighth stage is temporary and sporadic in nature. Further, it needs to be goal-oriented, meaning that collateral damages need to be kept low. The military action needs to always be viewed and evaluated in the light of the outlined goal of the operation.

To better conduct such operations and interventions, there should be rules, in order to prevent exploitation of such a situation for other interests that are not beneficial for the society experiencing such atrocities. For instance, if a civil war erupts in state A, other states should not seek to support the party that is furthering their own national interest. This might be a side which has pledged to enrich the helping nation after seizing power, for example. Rather, states should examine the situation thoroughly and make an assessment of where the roots of the conflict lay. Depending on the outcome of the examination, a solution should be crafted internationally. Such a solution can be very different depending on the case. It might be that the territory needs to be split up between two societies, a group needs to be relocated or that there just needs to be a diplomatic compromise between the parties to rectify the situation.

Under devletist intervention, the own interests need to be put aside, while the interests of the society that is subject to those large-scale problems need to be focused on. This can be very difficult in reality because the underlying motives of helping nations can never be fully known.

Here, we need to return to the sixth stage of foreign policy. On the international stage, states need to come together and cooperate more closely on these kinds of issues. Today, we already have the United Nations as a framework. However, in its contemporary form, it is not only hierarchical and biased towards (economically and militarily) stronger nations, but the structure of it is not fully designed to efficiently find technocratic solutions to such problems. It rather functions as a forum for such strong nations to further their interests. It needs to be reformed into an organisation that creates an environment of trust. This is only possible with many nations adopting devletist systems and a solid basis within each stage of foreign policy. We might be inclined to think that this would not suffice to create such a productive environment to tackle international problems because of our past experiences with nations behaving selfishly. But Devletism aims to rectify the normative understanding that led states to behave in such a selfish and destructive way. It creates a space for each state to become productive within its own boundaries and goes beyond the detrimental considerations of power and comfort. It is a system that pushes nations into maturity. A community of mature states will inevitably come together in a productive way and craft a framework of efficient international policymaking; simply, because the structure of Devletism will create an awareness that the devletist goal is of a much higher nature than the selfish goals that guide international state behaviour, today. Only then coordinated, streamlined and effective help of failing nations based on solidarity is possible – even militarily.

In order to illustrate this point, we can draw an analogy to our personal lives because the dynamics on the individual level can also be applied to the aggregate level of societies. A person who has found her special trait and is not only developing it but also translating it into real world outcomes, will develop a certain degree of confidence because she is experiencing true fulfilment. With this feeling of fulfilment, this person will not be inclined to interfere with the fulfilment of other people because there is nothing that the other person could add to this fulfilment. Either you are fulfilled or you are not. Hence, this person gets rid of detrimental traits, such as envy and narcissism. People who are not fulfilled, and therefore not at peace with themselves, usually chase material goals to fill the void their inability to experience fulfilment has created. However, these material things will never lead to a feeling of fulfilment which makes striving for material goals a never-ending endeavour into psychological misery. This is also the reason why the contemporary economic order is so successful in promoting luxury: the political systems of today do not help us to reach fulfilment.

While engagement in genuine knowledge production is inexhaustible in a fulfilling way, chasing material aspirations is inexhaustible in a destructive way. States act in the same way. Devletist states aim to incorporate their special trait (culture) into societal conduct, in order to progress as a nation. Non-devletist states will always merely chase more comfort and power, without ever being home to a fulfilled society. Accordingly, there will always be outward-looking agendas of such states, while devletist states will always progress with a domestic focus.

Viewing this devletist behaviour within the setting of an international organisation, we can now understand why such a setting is unlikely to be misused for exploiting other states or furthering individual states' interests at the cost of other states. Then, helping states in exceptionally hard times will produce positive outcomes and we can reasonably expect that states will mutually reduce their downside risk of systemic failure by crafting an environment of genuine solidarity. The international stage within a devletist world is, therefore, inherently productive, positive and enriching. There cannot be mistrust because the goal of all states is the same and any other goals are of lesser value. Since the direction of genuine knowledge production is universal, there are naturally no conflicting national interests. Every state aims to reach this point of understanding the objective truth through genuine knowledge production. The only difference is that every state is taking a different path because of the cultural uniqueness of each society.

Chapter XXII

About the Environment as a Policy Field

Our environment shapes our behaviour. This statement can be applied to every interpretation of environment. Whether we talk about our social surroundings, the nature or the physical environment we live in; if these surroundings are of high quality, so will we be. In this chapter, the roles of the environment (in the sense of nature) and urban planning are being discussed. Both aspects were much underrated throughout the history of politics. However, they constitute an own policy area under Devletism and being treated as equally important to the other policy fields with exception of education. Two factors serve as the pillars of this importance. First, it is the underrated potential of increasing productivity of people through harmony with nature. We should not make the mistake of limiting productivity to the economic realm, but also view it from the perspective of developing our special traits. Clean, positive and aesthetic environments will aid our efforts to reach our personal best.

Second, every single problem of mankind stemmed from the unacceptance of our inferiority to nature. Wars, resource exploitation and mass consumption are all born out of an implicit belief of being superior to nature. The assumption that the inorganic, as well as organic world, is made for humans to use is a thought of the lowest quality. Neither animals nor plants and stones are subordinate to the human – let alone are they existent to serve our existence. When we use them, we need to use them with this awareness which requires, but also reinforces, respect towards nature. In the greater context of the universe, we are not different from a piece of dust and we must act accordingly, which means that if we are to utilise a piece of dust, it must be used in a way that extracts maximum utility in the light of genuine knowledge production. If we are using stone and wood, they should be used in the way that will add maximum value to our goal of reaching a higher understanding of the universe.

Beginning with the environment, policymaking needs to aim to maintain a harmony between humans and nature. The very first step is to acknowledge that we are a part of nature and not the master of it. Our planet will surely outlive our species, just as some plants and animals might. However, if we want to prolong our existence as a species, we need to accept that we are merely a minor part of a complex system that can more dynamically adapt to our existence than we can to the existence of this planet. Such an acknowledgement is not merely expressed in words, saying that we respect nature and its laws, but in action. An important first step towards this acknowledgement is taken with the adoption of the thought that our purpose of existence is to strive for a better understanding of the objective truth. A second important step is then taken by understanding the way in which we can come closer to this objective truth is to find our special trait, develop it and produce real-world outcomes within that very field we are gifted in. The third step is to do this in an efficient way. Here, the factor of environmental protection starts to become more apparent because it is important that we use the given resources efficiently. This efficient use can be split up into two aspects.

First, it means that we must use regenerative resources in a way that they can still outgrow our demand. Water is a perfect example. Even though there is a certain amount of renewable water resources, our demand must be considerably less than the renewal rate, to allow the ecosystem to make use of those resources, too. In the example of wood, our demand or rate of deforestation must be significantly below the level of newly growing trees. Only by doing so, we can ensure that we will be able to obtain those resources in the future as well as not jeopardising the fragile balance of our ecosystem. We are not the only species that is dependent on these resources, meaning that we need to curb our consumption. Second, efficient use of resources also means that we must be mindful of the purpose of use. Today, the vast number of products is no less than overwhelming in a negative way. Not only that, the number of products increased greatly, but also the variants of every single product. Even though a soap block is enough to clean ourselves, today there are thousands of differently smelling shampoos, all of which need to be produced, packaged and recycled. In the end, the main purpose of those different shampoos is that we feel a little bit more comfortable. The outcome of a cost-benefit analysis, in the light of the environmental burden against the value for genuine knowledge production, would be more than catastrophic. Unfortunately, we can apply this very analogy to countless other cases of today's economic and political landscape.

The main measure that would reduce the burden on the environment is to reduce consumption. This theme should sound quite familiar when we think back at the chapters on the devletist economy. Since economic behaviour is the main driver of environmentally destructive dynamics, it is the task of the relevant authorities within the policy fields of economy and environment to aim for reduced consumption and that the remaining consumption is guided by the principles of long-lasting product life cycles and the use of high-quality material. But how can we achieve a functioning balance between consumption and environmental protection? Protecting our ecosystem is essential for our survival as a species. Accordingly, when trying to achieve a balance between consumption and the environment, any potential compromise between those two need to be made on the side of consumption. Where this is not possible, the compromise needs to be relocated to the price. For example, building clean, safe and sustainable production facilities is much more expensive than profit-maximising facilities because they require higher standards and are subject to stricter rules that need to be enforced. From building the facility at a location that minimises interference with nature, over implementing sustainable supply chains, to usage of sustainable materials and setting up proper waste management systems, the costs of such a facility are far greater than the costs of facilities that solely focus on quantitative production output. Also, resource procurement and the energy infrastructure are going to be more expensive because they will have to be optimised in an environmentally less burdensome way. All in all, the cost of production is increasing and with it the price of the produced goods. Therefore, the production of many products with minor value to the consumer will become non-profitable because the increased prices exceed the expected value. Consumers will make more conscious decisions about what they really need and want to afford.

Environmental policymaking is mainly concerned with setting and updating the quality standards of production and monitoring the implementation of such standards. Just to give another example, the production of meat would then be subject to standards such as space requirements for animals, regulations on fodder quality, maximisation of lifespans of animals and comprehensive ethical rules on the transportation and slaughter of animals. Mass production of meat will then no longer be possible, and the prices will increase. Consumers will then adapt their consumption behaviour according to the prices. In the light of environmental policymaking, the responsible authorities will need to constantly monitor whether producers adhere to the rules. Infringements need to be harshly punished, to establish this approach to environmental protection as an integral part of our normative thinking. Especially, the transition from the current consumerist societal behaviour will be quite difficult because the increased prices will prevent people from maintaining their current consumption rate, leading to temporal dissatisfaction. Over time, however, people will adapt their thinking and discontent will decrease. Because environmental protection was neglected throughout much of the industrial revolution and rise of the modern consumerist economy, economies were able to grow above the rates that would be objectively sustainable and healthy. Now that the ecosystem is rapidly changing, and affecting humans more radically, we need to urgently rethink the human-nature relationship. However, because this will reduce economic performance in the short run, the political system needs to enforce environmental protection even against popular discontent.

Chapter XXIII

Urban Planning

While environmental policymaking is generally rather passive because monitoring and reporting are the main tasks of the relevant authorities, urban planning is much more proactive. Further, while environmental protection is a universally approached aspect within this policy field, culture-based policymaking is a more central theme in urban planning. Here, policymaking is concerned with crafting aesthetic, sustainable and positive living spaces that incorporate the distinct architectural culture of the society. Not only does a clean and warm atmosphere reduces stress, increases productivity and quality of life but it also reduces criminality and fosters societal inclusion. The design of cities, towns and villages can, therefore, be seen as a key component of the societal infrastructure.

A suitable comparison is the function of the canvas for a painting. Surely, you can paint a picture on any canvas, but the quality of the canvas will determine the quality of the painting. So, it is in the case of urban planning. Since a dirty, hectic, stressful or dull living space is creating divisions between social and economic groups, urban planning needs to establish a high standard of quality for all citizens, in order to achieve the exact opposite of a dirty, hectic, stressful and dull living space.

Now, culture-based policymaking plays an incredibly important part here. At the most fundamental level, the societal organisation is an important determinant of which direction urban design is going to develop in. The general divide is to be made between collectivist and individualist societies. Collectivist societies are the clear majority in the world and are characterised by a high degree of social proximity and interaction among their members.[58] The interaction with other humans, in all kinds of relationships, is very important to the members of such a society. Concepts, such as family and friendship but also the interpersonal relationship with colleagues at the workplace, play central roles in the lives of people from collectivist societies. In addition to merely prioritising these relationships and interactions, people, to a certain degree, define their own identity through their relationships to other people. Wanting to be a good daughter within the normative framework of the family, for example, plays an important part of that person's behaviour and world thoughts, both shaping the identity of the person.

Individualist cultures think and behave differently. Again, to varying degrees, members of such a society perceive themselves as independent organisms. Social relations can be described as rather loose ties to other people and interaction with them

---

[58] Societies that are traditionally labelled as *the West* are the only truly individualistic societies in the world.

remains comparatively superficial. Within such societies, people build their identities around their personal experiences which they are also keen on experiencing in an exclusive manner, meaning that people in such societies often distance themselves physically and mentally from their social surroundings to experience certain things on their own. Based on these experiences, these people define their preferences and normative framework, which they also defend and hold on to in the course of social interaction. Collectivist people are rather lenient in seeking social harmony, which might include compromise on the personal side. Individualist people seek personal harmony or balance, even though this can create social disharmony or even conflict.

In terms of urban planning, this is an important aspect to figure out, because the living spaces need to be created according to the nature of that very society. In collectivist societies, living space does not need to be abundant because most of the time collectivist people are going to spend their time outside of their homes, interacting socially at different venues. Because this type of interaction plays an important role, they are naturally diversifying the range of activities and venues, to keep social interaction attractive. Therefore, cities in collectivist societies need to offer a wide range of social activities, while living space can be compromised. Since collectivist people are spending very little time at home, it is not important that their homes offer a lot of room to pursue personal interests. Rather, the public city spaces need to offer the comfort of a home.

Of course, cities need to be kept clean, and the architecture needs to be aesthetic, while being reflective of the respective society's architectural culture and history. However, especially in collectivist societies, it is important that there is no car traffic in the city centres because the noise and pollution are counterproductive to the creation of a cosy environment. To make up for the missing car traffic, public transportation needs to be greatly improved. Rail transportation must be the main means of intracity transportation. The reason for it is that it is comparatively silent, energy-efficient and can carry a lot more passengers than busses, for example. Further, there needs to be a lot of public spaces, such as parks, beaches and plazas because people will spend most of their time there. Accordingly, it is important that the municipalities make sure that there is a sufficient amount of garbage cans, public restrooms and free drinking water fountains. By doing so, the municipality takes care of the most basic needs and fosters a positive environment. In addition to serving the needs of the collectivist society, the aesthetic and sophisticated design of the devletist collectivist city will add to societal progress because people will be much happier and, therefore, more productive, adding to the pace of societal development.

The situation is different in individualistic societies. Here, people are much more focused on themselves. Social interaction is mostly planned and rarely spontaneous. For the most part, individualistic people spend their time at home, which is why they require more space there. If individualistic people live in limited spaces, they tend to develop mental illnesses which, at the aggregate level, harm the society as a whole. However, living space is a very limited and highly precious asset of nations. To make up for the bigger homes of individualistic people, the cities need to be considerably smaller. Rather than having extensive city centres and venues for social activities, those places should rather be limited to a necessary minimum. Due to the social structure, people will live more dispersedly, which requires more individual traffic. Cars, therefore, are going to be used a lot more than in collectivist societies. This requires a suitable infrastructure. However, there needs to be a balance between an extensive infrastructure and environmental protection.

This leads to a point around which both types of societies should structure their urban planning. Whether the society is collectivist or individualistic in nature, the living spaces of people should always be limited to a designated city, town or village area, meaning that they are enclosed and concentrated living spaces for humans, though not hermetically isolated. Humans should only be allowed to live within the borders of the city, town or village. Outside of the borders, the wilderness prevails until the next city, town or village begins. Nonetheless, there need to be sufficient green spaces, such as parks and forests, within the human settlings, but the aim of such an organisation is to allow the ecosystem to retain vast areas where there is almost no human intervention. The settlings are connected by highways and ports as well as airports and railways, but our way of living should not consist of stretched out settlements. Expansion of the settlements, which is inevitable in the light of a growing population, must be subject to parliamentary approval requested by the respective municipality.[59] A great advantage of such a settling policy is that the burden on the nature is concentrated in the populated areas, while the rest of the lands is nearly free from human intervention. Because nature can easily adapt to such a divide, a balance can be established relatively quickly and maintained as long as humans respect the divide.

Another universal aspect, that must be applied to collectivist societies in the same way as it is applied to individualistic societies, is sustainable management of the settlements. It is important that these enclosed settlements are managed in a resource-efficient way. Especially water is the main resource that needs to be reused as much as possible. Moreover, the municipalities should put an increased focus on keeping the

---

[59] This must happen on a regional basis and not for individual building projects. When the municipality plans to expand over significant areas and has valid reasons to do so, parliamentary approval needs to be sought.

settlements clean. Public spaces must be cleaned accurately by the municipality, but the owners of buildings must be forced to keep those buildings clean and properly maintain them. Further, they also continuously need to upgrade the buildings in terms of sustainability standards, to ever-increase their energy-efficiency and disaster-resilience. These legal requirements help to reduce the burden on the environment, which prolongs our existence as a species. Simultaneously, it creates the need to find more innovative solutions to increase efficiency together with a growing population and an increasing demand for higher standards of living, effectively spurring technological and scientific advance.

In total, the key element of urban planning is that the settlings of humans are concentrated and not dispersed. Within those settlings, the use of resources must be highly efficient, in order to accommodate population growth. Further, policymaking here is concerned with designing the social infrastructure according to core cultural properties of the society. What is universally applicable for all settlings is that they need to be kept clean and be subject to aesthetic standards of the society's architectural culture. Combining these aspects, policymaking in all other areas will be facilitated, due to the positive subliminal effects on the subconscious of the citizens. Productivity is thus increased because of the increased quality of life within the human settlements. Translating these principles onto the global stage, they will greatly reduce the burden that is currently being placed on the ecosystem. Additionally, it will extend our life span as a species significantly, while leaving room for healthy growth rates of our population. One might argue that the outlined measures are too invasive in relation to personal freedom, because such an urban design will need much central planning. However, since considerations around urban planning transcend personal interests and need to be holistically approached, there needs to be extensive regulation, in order to improve this aspect of societal life from the level of societal interest.

Chapter XXIV

The Devletist Welfare State

Moving on to the fifth policy area, another key element of devletist policymaking is the field of social welfare policies. These are rather new concepts within the realm of statecraft but have not only been integral parts of many political systems over the last century but also proven to be useful, if not necessary, additions to the proper functioning of states that have reached a certain point of development. While social welfare is a redistributive process concerned with levelling out social and economic differences, to enable more equal opportunities for all members of the society, social security describes a system of insuring members of the society against social and economic risk. Both play an important role in reducing systemic societal risk because they increase the rate of socio-economic inclusion. Because the benefits that people derive from those two policy mechanisms help them to reach or regain a certain socio-economic status, the amount of people who are burdensome to the political system through failure is kept low. Naturally, people who have experienced social or economic shocks recover considerably slower and fail more frequently within systems where the welfare system is rather underdeveloped. Such shocks and setbacks eliminate more people from the process of genuine knowledge production as well, which negatively affects the overall societal effort to advance. The negative effects are composed of two different aspects. The most obvious effect is that people who have experienced shocks are mentally and financially occupied with rectifying their situation, which removes them from the process of genuine knowledge production – potentially for years. However, if the situation is especially bad and people fall into homelessness, drug addiction or criminality, they will also proactively drag down people who are working on societal progress.

Looking at this policy field from this perspective alone, it becomes clear that social welfare and social security need to be part of devletist policymaking. One of the core premises of Devletism is that the society as a whole is progressing, which is an inherently inclusionary approach. Further, Devletism aims at enabling all people to find their special trait and also give them the opportunity to develop it. Some people are, unfortunately, not born into the best circumstances from a social or economic perspective, giving them a disadvantage from the start. However, these disadvantages need, where possible, to be artificially flattened out by the political system because such a person's special trait is not worth less than other people's. If those people are not assisted, they will have a much harder time to find and develop her special trait. Social welfare is levelling out these kinds of conditions, in order to maximise societal progress through inclusion.

Now, this topic in particularly is subject to much debate since it is seen as a crucial point over which the contemporary political divisions are defined. Whereas the so-called "political left" is favouring the implementation of social welfare policies, the "political right" is opposing these kinds of policies, though to varying degrees. The cause of the divide between the two perspectives is grounded in economic considerations at the superficial level. Social welfare is provided through state funds, which consist of taxes. Here, the usually economically better equipped political right is opposing the use of this tax money as financial aid to economically weaker members of the society. Of course, the arguments can be very different here. Some argue that they do not want to pay for other people's advantage. Others, in turn, argue that the funds can be used in different ways to facilitate economic growth. Yet others are concerned about public debt, arguing that the financial resources allocated to other socio-economic groups would be better used to reduce debt. On the other hand, the political left favours redistribution of societal wealth, due to a humanistic view. They argue that every person is entitled to a life with as little material problems as possible. In their view, people sometimes are unlucky in regard to the conditions under which they grew up or experience unforeseen shocks that disintegrate them from society. But also at the most basic level, when a company is bankrupt and the employees struggle to find new employment elsewhere, the social security benefits prevent deeper cuts into the budget of people. Through social welfare and security, the left believes, society becomes fairer and fosters equality.

On the technical level, however, both views are concerned with only one thing: social status. The political right generally consists of wealthier people, as mentioned before. Next to them, also people with high job security tend to sympathise with right political ideologies. What we understand as the political right is merely a description of a less economically interventionist state. If such an economically deregulated state is politically authoritarian, we call it a "conservatist state". If such an economically deregulated state is libertarian, we call it a "neo-liberal state". Even though they have different approaches towards socio-political issues (although they tend to be rather socially exclusionary), both share the view that members of the society should be as financially free as possible. That means that taxes should be minimised and preferentially there are no additional social welfare and social security measures that would be compulsory. Defending such a view is particularly attractive when the personal financial situation is an advantageous one, which is the case with many holders of the right political view. Such a non-interventionist policy environment would mean that the financial burdens laid on those people by the state would lead to a situation where they are even better-off financially. As contemporary political systems highly favour financially stronger members of society, more funds will equal more means of development for those wealthier people. This is due to the consumerist structure of contemporary societies, which is a result of the design of political systems that aim to increase comfort and not aim to engage in genuine knowledge production, as discussed earlier. Therefore, the political right does not desire to further increase the personal standard of living as a personal preference but to maintain the social distance to the economically weaker actors as it grants them a higher status within society overall.

On the other side, the political left is concerned with the very same problem of the social distance to the political right. However, it is keen on decreasing the distance to the political right because they are, on average, in a comparatively worse financial situation. Nonetheless, the political left is subject to the same consumerist structures of contemporary political systems which means that its worse financial situation, which does not have to be bad in absolute terms, leads to a less favourable position in social terms.[60] While the political right does not consider such an order to be negative because they are on the side that is clearly profiting from it, the political left perceives this

---

[60] We have seen earlier that wealth is relational as it requires an external point of reference which the own wealth can be measured against. We can also reformulate *wealth* into *financial power* and get the same result.

structure as a problem. Both materially and immaterially they are perceived to be weaker, compared to the political right. Materially, this should be quite clear because it was already stated that the political right is generally wealthier.

Immaterially, the political structure with the comfort focus is creating the perception that the political left is worse-off because the measurement of success within the current political order strongly correlates with quantity of financial means. While the political right has more means to potentially engage in genuine knowledge production, the left has comparatively fewer means, which reinforces this perception of inferiority. It is, therefore, in the inherent interest of the left to redistribute capital within society through welfare programs, in order to reduce the social distance to the right. Further, social security policies prevent the political left from falling farther behind the political right. While these arguments are also used within the political discourse of the left, they mainly focus on framing these measures in a normative way, stating that welfare and social security promote fairness and higher quality of life. On the other hand, the political right defends that within the structures of the deregulated market the conditions for success are already somewhat levelled, arguing that success, which is wrongly equalled with financial capacity, is solely dependent on the intensity of work put in by the participants in the economy.

However, because we know that within the contemporary system of aspired ever-increasing comfort, building wealth is considerably easier for already rich people. This wealth is translated to their social surroundings, enriching socio-economically similar people. This is already invalidating the argument of the political right that the members of society strive for success under equal conditions in the free market.

The devletist argument in favour of welfare is not built around considerations of fairness or social status, but – how else could it be – around the notion of genuine knowledge production. It cannot be denied that people are subject to very different environments and paths of life. Some are more fortunate in that they are facing more favourable conditions of development, while others will have a hard time to get to the point of truly engaging in genuine knowledge production as they have more existential hurdles to overcome. Social welfare within Devletism tackles these issues, to extract maximum value from each and every member of this devletist society.

First of all, devletist welfare policies need to ensure that all students face equal conditions at school because education is the heart of devletist thinking and the key to any nation's success. This means that less fortunate students will need to be supported financially but also immaterially. At the most basic level, students with a weaker economic background should be subsidised with working materials and in some cases even with high-quality clothes, if necessary. Any school, regardless at which education level, must provide students with a positive atmosphere. Merely having cosy buildings and friendly and fair teachers will not suffice. Students need to feel fully safe and welcomed in schools and having to face problems procuring the necessary working materials or attending classes with dirty clothes will quickly lead to social exclusion and reduced self-esteem. Also, whenever field trips or other events that require students' parents to bear the costs are organised, every student should be included and kept mentally far away from dealing with problems arising from their socio-economic background which they do not have any control over. Devletist social welfare must ensure that.

Further, unemployment benefits for short-time unemployed people should be put in place as well, in order to bridge the financially difficult period until a new job is found. Moreover, benefits granted to disabled people must also be included in the welfare system. They are important because disabled people are not less capable of producing genuine knowledge than non-disabled people. Only in cases of extreme cognitive disability, people will not be able to add to the progress of society, but this is seldom the case as most disabled people can equally well find and exercise their special trait, contributing to societal progress. The devletist state must ensure that they are in a situation that allows them to do so by providing them with the necessary financial support and removing as many barriers to their development as possible.

Focusing more on the efficiency aspect and less on the inclusionary dimension, devletist welfare systems need to craft meaningful retirement schemes. Even though people within devletist societies will mostly work in fields in which they are intrinsically interested in and, thus, are likely to continue their respective occupations until a high age, Devletism needs to ensure that their personal fulfilment endeavour does not end with their professional career, due to lacking financial means.

Even though there are different models that can serve as a solid basis for such a system, one of the best tools the state can utilise is the investment fund. Under such a system, the mandatory payments to the retirement scheme flow directly into a state fund which is extensively investing the capital. The generated returns are then paid to the eligible recipient. Now, this has the following effects: first, the retirement benefits that people will receive are much higher than those payments that can be paid within the framework of other systems because the invested capital is increasing in value rather than stagnating or even losing value, due to inflationary pressures. That alone is a strong argument in favour of state funds as a central part of retirement schemes. However, this has an additionally amplifying effect. Due to the large amount of capital that flows into the fund, the state can effectively invest in its own economy and, accordingly, boost economic conduct. Not only does this create overall wealth within the nation but it also reduces the downside risk as continued capital flows into the economy are ensured.

Next to the retirement scheme, another crucial pillar of welfare are matters related to public health. Now, the field of health is traditionally structured in a monopolistic way. Even in the very early days of humankind, only a limited number of people were exercising professions in this field and were often subject to formal or informal approval of the members of the respective community or society. Not only is the scientific field of medicine a complex one but matters that are related to health are sensitive. Still, considerations of survival constitute our most fundamental instinct and health is directly linked to this instinct of survival. Our health condition directly influences our chances of survival. Resolving health issues, therefore, is important to us and we tend to be sensitive when making decisions related to our health which includes who to trust when consulting a professional.[61] Because of the important of health in our lives, states mostly overtook the monopoly in this scientific field and incorporated it in their workings as a central aspect. It has become a central part of the societal infrastructure that the state needs to administer, however, in some states the benefits that are granted to the citizens in

---

[61] This is a suitable example to illustrate that we do not make decisions randomly, as discussed in Chapter VI.

matters of public health are insufficient to be considered as truly beneficial.

Some systems are highly inefficient, due to the great influence of corporate actors. These lobby for more favourable economic conditions within the fields of health insurance and medicine supply. Other systems fail to provide public health services to the whole society as economically weaker actors are structurally excluded. Though it is not openly communicated that economically weaker people are not sufficiently covered and, thus, often socially side-lined, the structures simply do not allow for them to access the most fundamental services, such as calling an ambulance or giving birth to a child under professional supervision.[62]

Health considerations pose great barriers to the effective and efficient process of knowledge production. Not only does the actual cases of illness and injury keep people from developing but when people live under constant fear that a health issue would disrupt their already fragile financial situation, the quality of their work will decrease, too. Devletist states, therefore, need to have

---

[62] If such a health system is solely discriminative through the economic variable and enables equal chances of economic success to all the members of the society, it can be viewed as a culturally aligned policy direction. However, since contemporary political systems tend to be discriminatory in a multitude of ways, the difficulties the disadvantaged within the society face when trying to gain access to health care are greatly more severe.

comprehensive public health systems which include extensive and unconditional health insurance.

While there are many ways to build such a system, the core aim of a properly functioning system is to eradicate any doubts and feelings of insecurity on the side of the citizens in matters related to their health. Citizens must be able to consult a doctor and receive the proper medicine and therapy without having to worry about economic or even social barriers. Unfortunately, the monopolistic nature grants actors within this field considerable economic advantages which can easily be exploited. Hospitals, insurers and companies in the fields of medical technology and pharmaceuticals can use their strategic position to extract economic advantages from a state that is concerned with providing encompassing benefits to its citizens. Accordingly, tying all hospitals and insurers to the state can be a feasible way to circumvent inefficiencies in this field. In the case of medical technology, this is much more difficult because it falls rather under economic conduct and the innovative aspect might not develop according to its true potential if centrally managed. However, here suitable normative standards and guidelines can help to reduce economic exploitation. Such regulations need to be applied to pharmaceutical companies, as well. Regarding hospitals and health insurances, the state should, however, administer these, in order to prevent goal displacement through privatisation.

There are many more policies, systems and mechanism that can be introduced under the umbrella of the policy field of welfare. What is important to consider when crafting social welfare frameworks, is the focus on enhancing conditions of genuine knowledge production for all members of society. It is the state's responsibility to design suitable measures that create an environment in which all people are able to find their special trait, develop it and translate it into outcomes. Any person who is not able to do so is preventing the society to advance at its highest rate.

Another aspect that is related to this efficiency-driven approach to the policy field of welfare, is that the policies need to be sensitive to the socio-cultural circumstances of the nation. As cultures highly differ, it is important that welfare policies are designed in a way that extracts maximum value within the context of the social structure of that society. For example, welfare policies tend to be much more comprehensive in collectivist societies, compared to systems in individualistic societies, because the feeling of belongingness is stronger. Whereas people in individualistic societies would have rather negative views on redistributive policies, people in collectivist societies are less averse towards redistributive policies. This is because the common identity is stronger in such societies, which leads people to be more supportive of mutual help – even when managed through the state.

Again, the main goal is to provide help to those who have more or greater barriers to face on their path to finding their special trait or, if they found it, to develop and utilise it. Doing so will enrich the nation as a whole, since more people are able to contribute to societal progress. Such an approach would, presumably, also be more attractive to potential opponents, for whom the argument of fairness and normative inclusion is usually too weak. Also, proponents of extensive welfare policies will be more receptive to limited welfare systems if they are effective in the light of genuine knowledge production. Technically, these concepts are useful policy inventions that help to address many intra-societal problems which makes them indispensable for any political system. Nonetheless, extensive welfare systems can be very dangerous, too. Not only could they potentially compromise economic efficiency of the state but in the long run they might even lead nations into decadency, which we have discussed before is the main cause of civilisational demise.

Chapter XXV

The Judiciary

The last policy area that this work is concerned with is the judiciary. Maybe the most striking characteristic of this policy field is that it is highly technical, yet completely grounded in normative structures. It can be described as the translation of qualitative and sometimes intangible notions into tangible outcomes, while also ensuring the survival of the ideas of Devletism in their material form. Here, the judiciary under Devletism is defined as a system of rules that are derived from a nation's cultural constitution, adjudicating intra-societal conduct of its members and institutions and ensures compliance through the imposition of penalties, all on the basis of rightfulness in the light of the cultural constitution. In other words, it is a translation of the identity of a people, outlined in the cultural constitution or manifesto, into a framework of tangible rules and regulations. In comparison to contemporary legal systems, devletist judicial systems focus on a more qualitative approach as the aspect of rightfulness is central to devletist thinking.

Today, many judicial systems are ineffective because they assess arising conflicts between legal persons in the light of their legality within existing legislative frameworks which gives politicians far-reaching powers. With small and gradual legislative changes over long periods, such legal systems become victims of goal displacement if they are not normatively anchored. Some governments in contemporary political systems are able to shift the political agenda strongly into directions that are far away from the cultural core of the society. A judiciary that backs any kind of change is a strong tool of such governments to consolidate new rules, which eventually may become customary. Moving back to the cultural core becomes especially difficult in such a situation and usually either leads to unrest and violent calls for change or the nation falls into demise. Surely, Devletism addresses this problem already with its voting system, structure of government staffing and the principles within the policy fields but also the judicial system needs to be designed in such a way that prevents the legal structures moving away from the core of the society's culture. Accordingly, building a legal system on the grounds of rightfulness is particularly important.

What is right and what is wrong can be difficult to agree on – especially, at a formal level. However, Devletism's biggest advantage is that it incorporates the idea of a cultural constitution, which already is an authoritative outline of what is considered right or wrong within a society. Naturally, this varies from society to society. Some societies have a particular aversion to financial crimes, like stealing or tax evasion. Within other societies, physical violence, such as smaller fights, is not considered to be too bad. Yet other societies approach violent acts of people more understandingly if they reactionary results from actions taken against the family of the offender. Just like the special trait of societies is individual, so is the understanding of right and wrong. Policymaking must understand this and the legislative workings of it must consider these aspects. However, if the judicial system is not able to properly adjudicate conflicts in the light of this cultural understanding of right and wrong, it will not be able to work effectively. Accordingly, the frame of reference for crafting a judicial system should not lay outside of the nation but at the heart of the own society.

Now, the challenge is to design a system that allows the legislative to craft policies independently but also one that incorporates a mechanism that checks whether the proposed legislature is aligned with the cultural core of the society. Further, it must be ensured that the judiciary is adjudicating conflicts on the ground of rightfulness. Intuitively, one would think of a mutual control mechanism that allows both sides, judiciary and policymaking, to remain in balance. Over time, however, such a mechanism will create a sense of competition between the legislative and judicative branches of the government, as such a mechanism can be viewed as a tool of one to exercise power over the other. To prevent that, both sides need to anchor the normative side of their workings to the cultural constitution of the nation. If the government is moving too far away from the norms and values, outlined in the cultural manifesto, the judiciary should be able to prevent the application of such legislation. In extreme cases, the military should retain the right to supersede the government, as it functions as the guardian of the nation, while only being a technical tool at the disposal of the government in times of regular state business. Other than that, the judiciary should not have any right to alter legislature, for it to remain hierarchically under the legislative branches of government.

However, a potentially useful mechanism, to ensure that new legislature and changes to existing legislature are in the sense of the cultural constitution, is the cooperation between judiciary and the legislative in outlining the proposal in a way that defines right and wrong for the specific case at hand. Here, the judicial precision of wording is useful to formulate clear guidelines for future application in the adjudication process of the relevant courts. On the other hand, the policymaking side can clearly communicate its intentions and aims with the proposed legislature. Once this outline of right and wrong within the process of policymaking is agreed upon, the judiciary has merely an implementing function. It then becomes a purely technical matter of making judgements within the agreed frame of right and wrong. As such, both sides channel their expertise into crafting understandable and functional legislature. Further, the application process in cases of legal conflicts becomes more effective. In contemporary systems, legal persons often look for legislative and linguistic loopholes to exploit. When legislature, however, is crafted in the light of right and wrong, also matters that are linguistically ambiguous can be assessed effectively because there is an understanding of what is acceptable behaviour or not, as well as how unacceptable behaviour in this context would be judged.

The major advantage of such an approach is that there is no need to account for every single potential situation where law is breached. Rather, it forms a broad legal space that is flexible and allows for contextual judgements. Let us assume that a person committed a murder in an attempt to protect another person from an assault. Within a society in which such crimes are heavily condemned, the murderer would most likely not be sentenced, and the legal procedure would likely be a short one because of the clarity of hierarchy between the normative principles that influenced the murder. In most contemporary legal systems, however, such a process would most likely be lengthy because it is grounded in the notion of legality and not rightfulness. Here, the hierarchy of relevant principles is less clear, often conflicting and an assessment is more difficult – even though the question of right or wrong is less ambiguous. Sometimes, crimes that are truly unacceptable in the light of the cultural core of the society remain unpunished, while people who are considered innocent within the cultural context are sentenced. This reduces trust in the judicial system, causes dissent and in the long run moves societies farther away from their cultural core. Accordingly, a universalist approach is least effective in the context of the judiciary because societies greatly differ in their perception of right and wrong.

Previously, it was stated that the judiciary should cooperate with the legislative branch in transforming the planned legislation into suitable frameworks of right and wrong. Further, it was stated that the judiciary is hierarchically below the legislative because it is applying the law and not crafting it. However, this does not mean that it should be subject to control – the contrary is the case. A properly functioning judiciary must be independent from the legislative, in order to be able to prevent it from misusing the judiciary for pursuing interests outside of the societal interest. Also, it is the most important precondition for unbiased workings of the judiciary, even though a fully unbiased judicial system is currently impossible to achieve. Since socio-economic biases cannot be fully eradicated, shielding the judiciary from political influences is all the more important. Throughout this work, many of the proposed measures aim at curbing the powers of the government as the potential human errors arising in policymaking are the greatest liabilities of a nation. Not only is the management of a nation creating incredible pressure on the politicians but it also opens great opportunities for personal enrichment. Most political systems to this day failed to provide structures that prevent just that.

However, whenever the judiciary became interconnected with politics, the societal decline greatly accelerated because politicians increasingly enriched themselves and shifted their focus away from working in the interest of the nation. By shielding the judiciary from political influence, it can be ensured that at least existing legislature is adjudicated in an effective way.

The final aspect of devletist judiciaries is the matter of punishments. Just as the laws of a nation are deeply rooted in the cultural core of the society, punishments, too, need to equally reflect the society's views of right and wrong. Today, most judicial systems utilise prisons as a form of punishment. Unfortunately, this is a completely unsuitable punishment for many societies in the world because it is an invention created in the context of individualistic societies. It reflects the normative assumption that the personal freedom is the highest good of a person and, thus, depriving people of this freedom is considered as a harsh punishment. Of course, some nations still apply the death penalty, which is, objectively seen, the harshest form of punishment, but the most commonly utilised form of punishing crimes remains prison.

As mentioned earlier, individualistic societies are strongly centred around the idea of personal freedom, though this is not so much the case in collectivist societies. Here, prison sentences are less effective because the personal freedom is not as highly valued as social contact, which is still given in prisons, due to social contact with fellow inmates. Punishments, accordingly, need to be equally reflective of the cultural core. This means that crimes that are considered especially harsh in the context of the respective society's normative framework of right and wrong must be punished in a suitable and not universal way. However, punishments should not merely be applied for the sake of punishing criminals, but need to be designed in a way that allows for a learning process. Where such a learning process is not possible, the punishment must aim to prevent a repetition of the crime or other crimes. This is because we must acknowledge that even criminals have a special trait and if they are removed from the process of genuine knowledge production, the nation is not developing at its true potential.

It follows that criminals need to be punished in a way that enables them to re-enter society as functioning members who add to the progress of the nation. Imprisonment is especially unsuitable in the light of genuine knowledge production because it removes people from engaging in genuine knowledge production, or at least makes it considerably more difficult for prisoners to do so. Moreover, they incur costs that the taxpayer is bearing, while this capital could be used more efficiently elsewhere. This is not to say that imprisonment is an outright useless way of punishing criminals, but it is certainly not the only way and in most societies a tool of secondary utility in the light of devletist judicial workings.

Chapter XXVI

Epilogue

We have now reached the final chapter of this work, which I would like to close with some concluding remarks. Our species faces some great challenges today as well as in the future. They are not greater or smaller than past challenges because they, too, arose from the specific circumstances of that time. The constant that remains, however, is our own nature. It is the driver behind any kind of progress achieved, but also the driver behind the problems that we face. Even though we cannot change our nature, we can try to understand it better and then go on to build structures that lead us to behave better. Certainly, politics has always tried to do so, based on certain perceptions of the world. In some periods, we were more successful, while our species also experienced phases in which progress was halted. Even in an ideal world, we will not always operate at full efficiency, unfortunately – simply, because one of the laws of the universe is that it moves in waves. Good times cause bad times, just as bad times cause good times. The key to a more fulfilling life is to adapt our behaviour to the movement of the waves and maybe reduce their fluctuations a little bit – removing them is impossible.

In its essence, Devletism is concerned with anchoring our focus on the purpose of our existence. It aims at keeping us on our path to achieving a better understanding of the universe. It is not a compromise between ideology, religion and egoism, but rather the only positive commonality between these three political drivers. It protects our inherent nature, challenges our personal limits and provides us with a plan to reach the deepest form of fulfilment. It reaches beyond our current understanding of the world as something temporary and limited, and connects the past with the future through the present. Devletism is inclusive and generous, but also demanding and uncomfortable. It does not end wars, famine or suffering but its principles provide guidance, shelter and hope. Because its goals lay beyond worldly and even spiritual considerations, every step in the light of genuine knowledge production brings us fulfilment.

But because our nature is so complex and unchanging, Devletism, too, will experience times of difficulty. It will be misunderstood and misused by some, just as any novel idea was; ironically, usually by those who benefitted from the fruits of those ideas the most. If the idea proves to be close to the unknown objective truth, it will, just as other ideas that are close to this truth, overcome those times – over and over again.

Even though this work is concerned with the devletist state, we can incorporate the ideas into our personal lives, too. At first, we need to start a journey to the deepest parts of our soul where we shall find the truth about ourselves by finding our special trait, our gift, our destiny. Once found, every step in the direction of our special trait will bring us fulfilment. It is the only way of exercising our being in the truest sense. All other goals, wishes, aspirations, needs and wants will be attracted to the person who is living in accordance with her true nature. Applied to the state, the nation which is moving along the lines of its true self will transform life within its nation into one of happiness, prosperity, peace, progress and fulfilment. On the path to developing into such a nation, great challenges lay ahead of us.

But a thought is like a plant. Planted in fertile soil and continuously watered, it will grow.

- Emre Şentürk